Portland, OR   Feb. 25, '10

Saving Magic Places

Bill –

May you have many magical adventures in Nature –

Happy B-day!

Ann (& Marc)

Saving Magic Places

EMILY EVE WEINSTEIN

Beau Soleil

publishing

Library of Congress Card Catalog Number: 2007934163

ISBN- ISBN-13: 978-0-9771978-9-7

First Edition, First Printing

Printed in the USA

10% Post-Consumer
Content

www. WeinsteinArt.com

Beau Soleil Publishing

ISBN 13- & 977 8 7

Emily P Weinstein
P.O. Box 3220
Chapel Hill, NC 27517

Acknowledgements

A special thank you to
those who helped greatly:

Mara Alperin
Marc Alperin
Wendy Bernhardt
Jeff Fisher
Patrick Grace
Wendy Jacobs
Jane Korest
Elaine Lite
Alice Griffin Myers
Mark Phillips
Norman Weinstein
and all the worker bees who
made *Saving Magic Places*
possible.

This book is dedicated
to active enviromentalists
everywhere.

Table of Contents

Introduction

I LOOKED FORWARD TO STARTING my new project, *Magic Places*, with great anticipation. I envisioned a year or two of painting vacation spots, remarkable gardens, and other oddities of man and nature.

My plans changed dramatically, however, when I learned that my first magic place was in jeopardy. 100 acres of pristine stream and forest located across the road from my studio were slated for development. Plans for the new subdivision involved altering natural stream beds, cutting old-growth forest, and destroying irreplaceable wildlife habitat. At this point, the project became *Saving Magic Places*, and what had begun as a simple artistic journey was transformed into something much bigger: an all-out battle to secure a corridor of contiguous, protected forest that extends for more than 35 miles. In the process, I learned that the spirit and will to protect our planet's threatened natural resources extend to millions of visionaries around the world.

Saving Magic Places tells the story of how one group of friends and neighbors struggled valiantly to protect local forest from demolition. The struggle began with a modest handful of people but quickly grew to involve thousands. The journey took many convoluted turns shaped by the personalities and talents of the many players who participated in noteworthy ways. As a participant in the project, the paintings and text represent my take on it all. Also included are the voices, recollections and viewpoints of others on the journey. By combining paintings with text, I hope to inspire and encourage readers to work to save the natural beauty around them. It can and must be done.

The appendices provide details, descriptions and information and offer advice and examples of how to proceed, and what to expect, with a project like ours. In addition, the final appendix offers useful contact information for those who are contemplating or are already on the way to committing to an environmental project.

Above all, the purpose of *Saving Magic Places* is to recognize and join the universal desire to champion and protect our natural world. This book invites its reader/viewer to be one with the growing multitudes who are saving magic places.

En Plein Aire ◆ EARLY SPRING ALICE AND I go down

the dirt road in walking distance of our homes. She plans on working in watercolor today; I've got a mess of oil painting supplies in my five-gallon bucket. I empty the bucket, then turn it upside down to make an outdoor studio. I have French easels, but prefer my lightweight makeshift setup.

Our subject is an antebellum farmhouse, circa 1842, surrounded by an established garden with buds just opening. Close by is a leaning shed which had been inhabited by an itinerant couple up until the 1940s. They murdered their landlord who owed them money and tied his mother up under the staircase of the main house.

Current residents, couple Liz and Ron, are garden designers, rock workers, artists. Liz brings us herbal tea. By 5 PM the sun is sinking, it's getting chilly, light is changing. I won't be back for a week as I'm going to New York. Before we store our supplies on the porch, Alice critiques my work, "Is that chair supposed to be floating? You have lots of work to do on the front half." It will have to wait.

The Shed   10" x 10"   Oil on board

Antebellum Farmhouse   30" x 30"   Oil on board

"A WONDERFUL COMMUNITY FOR ME IS ONE WHERE EVERY CHILD IS WITHIN WALKING DISTANCE OF A CREEK WITH TADPOLES."

Jane Korest, Open Space and Real Estate Manager

Operatic Frog   7" x 9"   Oil on board

Hart and Scarlet   14" x 11"   Oil on wood

Changes ❖ BACK FROM NEW YORK and down the dirt road, I'm greeted by Ron. "This land has been sold. all 100 acres to developers. We have a month to move. Our season has just begun. One month to dig up 1,000 plants and go somewhere. Where? I've been here 15 years. Maybe we'll go north. With 600 plants?" He speaks in a monotone. I visualize 200 McMansions erected over stream beds, oak groves gone, millions of animal homes destroyed.

I can't paint. Walking home, I see Vickie mulching new plants. Dobermans Hart & Scarlet bounce about. Vickie is devastated by the news but not altogether surprised. She agrees to go downtown and get the plat map. My neighbor Lisa is in her garden, too. I tell her. Despite it all sounding like a done deal, we decide we must try to protect what we can. We can count on fellow artist Alice and, we hope, the adjacent Stonegate Community; in terms of humans, they will be the most affected by this debacle.

4

Connections ◆ WITH MY NEIGHBORS LISA AND ALICE, we attend City Council meetings, first in support of the newly formed Arrowhead Neighborhood Group, then us, EANG (Erwin Area Neighborhood Group). The developer's rep is a friendly, dapperly dressed man who tells us how beautiful the development will be and how many trees will be saved, streams protected. He states that he lives in this area and cares. That same day I drive around photographing their nearby "beautiful developments" one scrawny twig planted in each front yard to replace the now largely slain old-growth trees. The streets are broad, the houses identical. That night Lisa sends out by email a strong call to action: WE NEED YOU NOW!!! TWO ARTISTS AND A TAG-ALONG GRAD STUDENT DO NOT MAKE UP AN ENVIRON-MENTAL GROUP!!!

Lisa's call to action works. Two days later about 15 come to our meeting. We plan strategy, but it is late, very late for this land. I think about where the displaced tenants can go. Around the corner and currently empty is a place where Alice and I occasionally paint, an ancient farmhouse on the Penny land. In paint-splattered clothes, with thoughts fresh in my head, I race to the house across the road from the deserted place, the Penny home. I ring the doorbell multiple times. A woman looking perplexed cracks the door. I explain, "I found you great renters. They'll transform the place. They are the gardeners needing to move because of the pending development. Oh, and by the way, I'm Emily Weinstein, the painter." Carolyn Penny then introduces herself. A month later Liz and Ron move into the large farmhouse, digging up and then transplanting over a thousand plants at their new home.

HOMES THAT DO NOT REQUIRE CUTTING DOWN TREES:

Henry's Brother   5" x 24"   Oil on reclaimed cedar siding

Sheila's Place   6" x 48"   Oil on reclaimed cedar siding

3 AM   5" x 24"   Oil on reclaimed cedar siding

Henry's   6" x 40"   Oil on reclaimed cedar siding

The Smith's   5" x 24"   Oil on reclaimed cedar siding

Emily Eve Weinstein

Boulder, Hollow Rock Creek   30" x 30"   Acrylic

Others ◆ HIKING WITH CHINA-DOG, we meet two amicable hound mixes. As the dogs play, I learn that their person, Jeff, is the executive director of the Tar River Land Conservancy. I tell him about our land battle. He is sympathetic but feels it's a done deal. When I get home I mention him to neighbor Wendy, who has taken a lead role in attempting to get an arborist on board, buffers increased, density reduced, and protective fencing around trees. She has been polite and cordial with the slick rep, way beyond my ability. About the time the city signs off, we get news of Duke University selling a portion of forest that we thought was protected. Maybe we are not too late for this one.

Meanwhile on the 100 acres, developers, once given the green light, immediately level 200 feet of buffer. No protective fencing, no change in density. The slick rep who claimed to be committed to the area has moved back to Texas. They declare they know nothing of agreements we had with their bamboozler. Ron, the caretaker of the forest for 15 years, borrows a portrait of the land from Alice to show town hall. Single-handedly this action, accompanied by his words, has slowed the operation down and protective fencing has since gone up.

Rock Wall, Hollow Rock Creek   10" x 10"   Oil on wood

Regrouping ❧ WE ARE MEETING at our common house with Becky Heron, County Commissioner, regarding Duke University's proposed sale of the 44 acres of forest land to developers. She points out that the land is adjacent to land that is part of the New Hope Creek Corridor and that there was a group of environmentalists twenty years ago dedicated to keeping the water as free from run-off as possible. Leading them was environmental heroine Hyldegard Ryals, now in the process of moving to a retirement community. This was a fight she may have to let pass, but with a quick call from Becky she is at the second meeting. And so is Jeff, without China's two dog friends. Wade and Carolyn Penny, Liz and Ron's new landlords, have been alerted, but they are headed to Scotland.

Jeff talks strategies for raising over $1,000,000 to buy the land, "To hell with requesting larger buffers. Let's just buy the land and then we will have really big buffers!" My attention lost, I doodle; they talk of a logo, a theme, *The Missing Puzzle Piece*. My doodle becomes our logo. I suggest AstroTurf pins to sell.

Wendy prefers they be given to those that pledge. Lisa wants yard signs and bumperstickers everywhere. Someone else suggests Burma-Shave type signs along the forest roads. In ten days we are calling an open meeting to get all on board for the New Hope Creek Park! Ten days to reserve the middle school's cafeteria, get yard signs and bumper stickers designed and printed. The Scrap Exchange donates sign materials and campaign buttons for attaching squares of Astroturf. Alice and I become a sign-painting factory. Deb Christie and I make 200 pins with the help of Wendy's kids, Eliza and Caleb. Phil and Nancy take over refreshments. People from neighborhoods across the Erwin area pitch in with various tasks. Wendy, Lisa and Jeff organize everything else. Deb places the announcement signs at intersections.

Hanging Rock of New Hope Creek   11.5" x 14"   Oil on reclaimed board

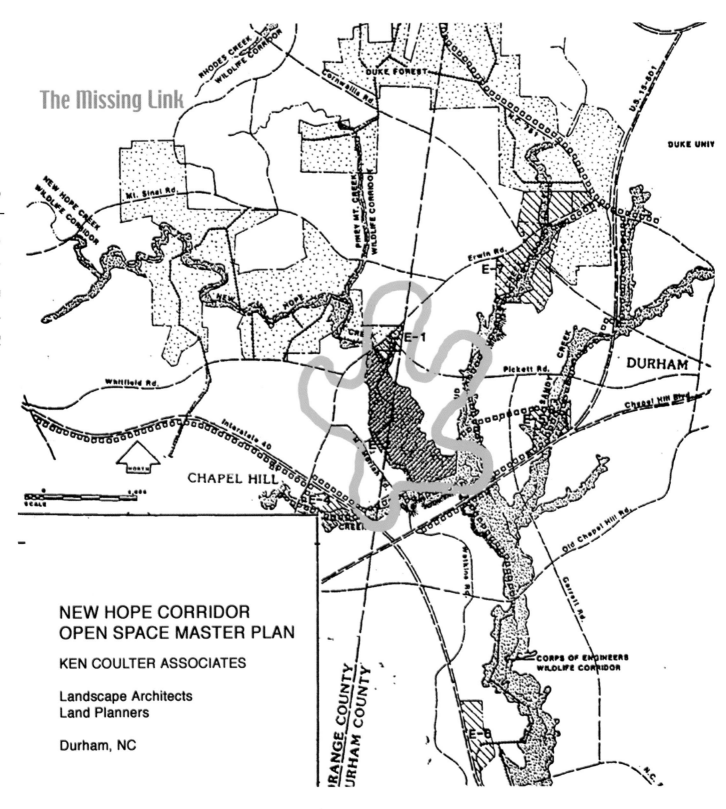

The Missing Link

NEW HOPE CORRIDOR
OPEN SPACE MASTER PLAN

KEN COULTER ASSOCIATES

Landscape Architects
Land Planners

Durham, NC

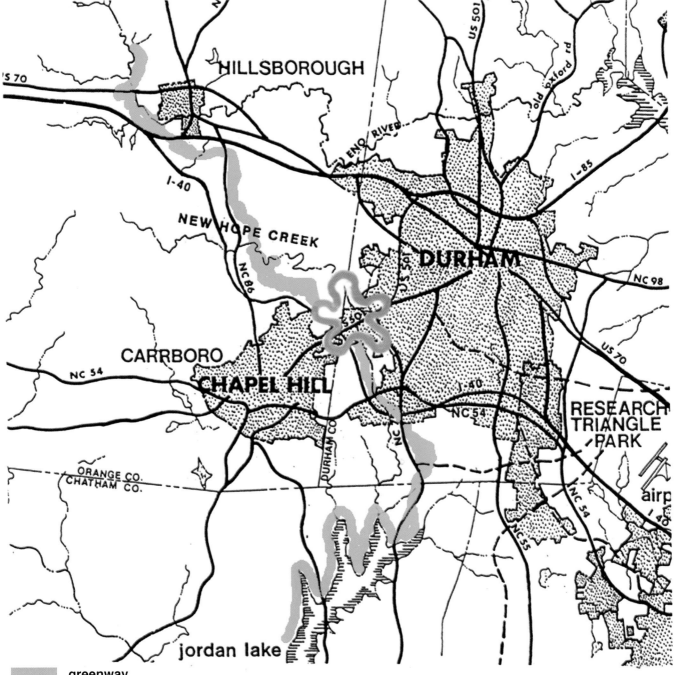

Emily Eve Weinstein

HILLSBOROUGH

US 501

old oxford rd

US 70

I-40

ENO RIVER

I-85

NEW HOPE CREEK

NC 86

DURHAM

US 501

NC 98

CARRBORO

NC 54

CHAPEL HILL

DURHAM CO.

NC 54

US 70

RESEARCH TRIANGLE PARK

ORANGE CO.
CHATHAM CO.

NC 54

NC 55

airp

jordan lake

 greenway

major bodies of water

rivers and major streams

city and town limits

major roads

VICINITY MAP   NEW HOPE CORRIDOR

The Big Night ❖ THE FOREST VIEW SCHOOL cafeteria is filling up fast. I am asking one and all to sign the petition. Alice is taking in pledge form after pledge form. Eliza is selling the stickers and yard signs as fast as she can take the money. Twelve-year-olds Caleb and Danny are outside directing traffic to the overflow parking lot. Our goal is to reach $100,000 in two months. Jeff does a power-point presentation. Wendy talks of how "once land is gone, it is gone forever. Now is our time to act." Becky Heron says a few words, followed by Hildegard, and then Wade Penny gets up to announce the jaw dropper: he and Carolyn are pledging $15,000 once we reach $25,000! The crowd explodes, the momentum is on. Twenty-five neighborhoods are already on board. At this point we have 70 pledges totalling more than $22,000!

Liz and Ron's at Night   12" x 12"   Oil on reclaimed board

End of the Road   11" x 14"   Oil on reclaimed board

Return to Normalcy, Kind Of ❖ LISA, THE GRAD student,
has to go back to school and I need to get some painting done. Fellow artist, Diane Burke, and I go to an unknown park. No one is there: no parked cars, no strollers, joggers or dogs. It is on the edge of the 15-501 bypass. My plan is to do a painting of natural and man-made merging. We park at the entrance. The narrow road winds down around a field toward park benches next to a swampy pond. Diane plans to investigate the rest of the terrain to find her painting spot. I stop her, pointing out a pile of litter in a ditch: many boxes of Paxil. There must be several hundred pills. After phoning the police from Diane's cell phone, we both set up our painting gear. I choose a scene of various evergreens in the foreground with a distant horizon and cars racing by. Their occupants have no idea we are here or that drugs have been stashed in a ditch.

Alice Griffin with her painting of the Sycamore
Cut-out
Oil on wood 12" x 7"

HOW WE GOT TO WHERE WE ARE,
I DECIDE TO INTERVIEW SOME OF THE KEY
FOLKS ON MY TEAM:

"ALICE, IT'S ALL A BLUR TO ME.
WHAT IS YOUR VERSION?"

Alice Griffin ◉ FOR ME IT STARTED IN EARLY SPRING
2004. We walked down a dirt road into what you said
was a "magic place." It was! There stood magnificent
old trees in a serene 102-acre forest; we disturbed a
herd of deer. I felt transported back home to the
Roanoke River lowlands that I love. I painted a majestic sycamore tree that day. Soon we learned all this was
to be altered forever. There was a rush by developers
to gain approvals before more protective ordinances
were enacted. Only limited data on the environmental
impact upon schools, roads, traffic, noise, air quality
(etc.) was required.

Incensed, I phoned Jim Wise, who was doing a
good job reporting the development surge in Durham,
about the developers having to estimate only the number of cars exiting daily. He quoted my consternation
about cars arriving at the already overused nearby
intersection. "What do they do then? Sprout wings
and fly?" Chagrined, I decided to keep quiet and work
behind the scenes from then on. The developer's rep
had asked to buy my painting of the sycamore. "I
need to see how things turn out," I told him. Well, we
spoke for that forest, but we lost it. I still have my
painting.

In the meantime you discovered surveyors in the-
woods on our southern side. The day after the Jim
Wise article appeared, Lisa sent out an SOS to Solterra

The Shed 9" x 12' Watercolor and pencil

and set up a meeting two days later with County Commissioner Becky Heron. EANG was formed with Wendy Jacobs as our articulate chair. Jeff Fisher pro-posed buying the Duke Forest land for a park or pre-serve. We were up and running in another fight for a forest.

Beeches in Fall
9.5" x 7.75"
Oil on wood

Judd Edeburn ● DUKE IS BLIND-SIDED BY THE GROWING MOMENTUM of the community to obtain this land. The resource manager of Duke Forest, Judson Edeburn, explains that in the late eighties the University did a comprehensive review of its land holdings, originally obtained in the 1920s and 1930s. All 8,000 acres were priority-listed under four categories, the last one the smallest and most isolated tracts of land, not used adequately and declared extraneous. These 44 acres, Mr. Edeburn explains, are isolated from the large tract across the road where major land uses occur, as with the Nicholas School of the Environment where Duke students learn hands-on about the different types of soils, tree species, the native flora and fauna, and those that are invasive imports.

The 44 acres would have continued in their undeveloped and uncontested state but for a builder seeking land to develop, who was directed to Duke's Scott Selig, capital assets manager. The land, though not advertised, was indeed available for purchase. However, it came with stipulations the builder must adhere to: the current zoning must not change, only existing infrastructure could be used and the name of the development must not be associated with Duke University. Seven acres of this parcel rest in Orange County, thus posing another limitation to the developer in that there will be no building on this portion because of Orange County restrictions. Talman Trask, the Executive Vice-President of Duke, recognizing the growing opposition to any portion of the New Hope tract being built on and is willing to listen. In a spirit of cooperation, Trask calls their prospective buyer in for a meeting. What would it take to buy him out of the current contract? Five hundred thousand dollars in recognition of Crosland's loss. The seemingly astronomical goal is now set at a million and a half dollars!

As Edeburn explains, the University likes the idea of maintaining open space but simply does not care to own it. However, as things turn out, the seven acres of the land in Orange County will not be developed. As part of Orange County's rural buffer, they are on the other side of the road. There are other tracts, though, within Duke's Residual Endowment Lands that are not contiguous to parts of the Forest and fall into that fourth category, namely, underused and extraneous land. Talman Trask works hard on behalf of everyone to arrive at an amicable solution, albeit an expensive one. There is a chance that these tracts may rest in their unhampered state indefinitely, but not necessarily so for those special 44 acres that are now very much in focus.

Judson Edeburn   Cut-out
Oil on wood 11.5" x 3.5"

Emily Eve Weinstein

Barry Jacobs ◉ THE ORANGE COUNTY CONNECTION TO DUKE... Like many that are working at obtaining the Duke parcel, Commissioner Barry Jacobs has a connection that goes back eight years. For one thing, Alice and I learn from him that Duke University is the largest landowner in Orange County. Just prior to his election in 1998, the three governments of Orange County, Chapel Hill and Carrboro had tried to obtain a section of Duke Forest within the Blackwood Division, as the University planned to sell it. The plan was to put a landfill there. Upon hearing this, Duke went to NASA suggesting a CO_2 Omissions Station, thus totally dismissing the three jurisdictions and their unattractive plans. Relations with Duke were strained at the time Jacobs was elected.

With Dave Stancil, Commissioners Steve Halkiotis and Barry Jacobs, all instrumental in creating Orange County's innovative Lands Legacy Program, sought to improve relations with the largest landowner of their county. With the idea of forging trust, they proceeded to obtain a portion of the Blackwood Division, which is now the McGowan Creek Preserve. From the improved position Stancil, Rich Shaw and Jacobs requested that Duke always come first to Orange County when they were divesting of land within the borders of the county. Duke agreed. Soon after, unrelated to Duke property but connected to the Eno River Park, 391 acres became available straddling both Durham and Orange Counties. A landfill was proposed of the construction and demolition waste variety, but with strong opposition from citizens and county commissioners, it was successfully blocked. Barry Jacobs, Durham commissioners Becky Heron and Ellen Reckhow, and Kate Dixon, then director of Triangle Land Conservancy, walked the land. It was decided then to submit a grant through the two jurisdictions at the Federal level. Their proposal, signed by representatives from two counties and two land trusts, creating a public-private partnership, was so excellent an idea, though rare, that significant grant funding was obtained.

Barry Jacobs with Truman & Ford
11.75" x 5.5"
Cut-out, oil on wood

The Little River Regional Park was the lynch pin inspiring this team of commissioners to work hard for the New Hope Creek Park. If two jurisdictions were viewed as enough of a remarkable novelty to work, why not four? At the same time that Duke was working with Crosland developers to purchase the New Hope Creek parcel, they had simultaneously contacted Orange County about the seven acres of this proposed deal in their county. This stipulation was written into the builder's contract. If Crosland did not buy the land, Orange County planned to buy the seven acres. After all, the University had contacted them. Unfortunately, Durham had not forged a symbiotic relationship with Duke as Orange County had.

In the Woods
11.75" x 8.25"
Oil on wood

Hildegard Ryals ◉ THE IDEA IS TO START OUT WITH what you want to save, not end up with leftovers! What is important is linkage, and that is why this forest is so important. To those that say it isn't so, I simply reply that if this is a hand, then this is the thumb. I'd worked with Hollister Whyte, a national figure in saving open spaces. He also advocated really admirable principles: working lands, timber, crops, connected forests, protected streams, cluster housing; in short, working with the land rather than against it. I got involved with preserving New Hope Creek and adjacent areas after meeting Margaret Nygard, the founder of the Eno River Association. She was moving a mill stone. Finding out about my work with Whyte, she said, "You must do something about New Hope Creek!"

The Creek is not dramatic like the Eno River, but it is interesting. It starts from the west as a mountain stream flowing into the slate belt to the sandy Piedmont. To protect this significant geology, we formed the New Hope Creek Corridor Advisory Committee. It is important to get the inter-jurisdictional cooperation of all four governments that stand to gain from the green corridor. This will also help greatly with grant writing—if we get to that point.

Hyldegard Ryals with
Typhoon & MeiLa
Oil on wood, 12" x 5"

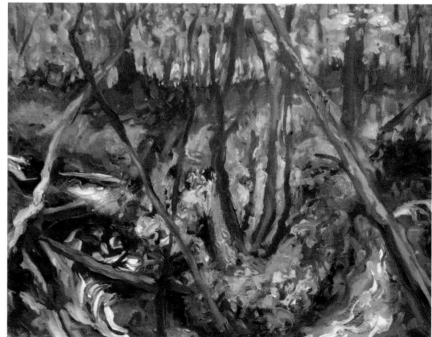

Hollow Rock Creek   8" x 8"   Oil on reclaimed board

Chairs   30" x 30"   Oil on wood

Chuck & Carol Eilber ◉ EM, YOU AND ALICE TOLD us about the surveyors down in the woods. Our neighbor, Kim, went to the planning department to get a copy of the new site plan. We point out drainage issues with the Development Review Board. The county engineer then notices that a tributary of the stream is not evident in the plan. This puts everything on hold as the area has to be re-surveyed. Four houses are bumped to allow for adequate stream buffers to suit the county. When the developers present their plan to the city, however, there is a good chance those four houses will make their way back into the plan. The city is more lenient. It looks likely the contract will go through, and to think we had resigned ourselves to the development that had just taken sail when this one landed on us!

Carol and Chuck Eilber
Oil on wood   12.5" x 6.25"

Eliza & Wendy   Oil on wood   12" x 6"

Wendy Jacobs ◉ WE HAVE ALL OUR MATERIALS READY: We have named ourselves Erwin Area Neighborhood Group (EANG), reserving the web name ErwinNeighbor.org. We are well organized before the public kick-off campaign January 24. We previously joined the Arrowhead Group, people working to remain in the rural tier, and then along comes the surprise of the Duke Forest land—a place we assumed was protected. December 8 we convince the county to invoke the right to implement a reservation of four months on this new plan that would no doubt end up destroying yet another precious tract of pristine green space in our area and have a negative impact on these tributaries of New Hope Creek. By the time this latest developer comes into existence, I am in touch with 19 neighborhood spokespeople. We have also developed relationships with elected officials, the local environmental groups are on-board, and we have a core group of work- horses. Jim Wise does a great article with color photographs, and the preserve-park concept devised by Jeff and Lisa, together with the Penny land, expands the vision. The Triangle Land Conservancy is the backing non-profit. We need all these pieces for a shot at success. At our kick-off event in January, we have no idea how many will show. So, when, 20 minutes early, people start trickling in and then, closer to the time, pouring in, it is very exciting. We sell our vision of the missing link, the missing puzzle piece: this tract is important; it needs to be saved.

(See Appendix **A**, page 79, for a continuation.)

Maddie by her Lily Pond   14" x 16"   Oil on antique wood

Cliffhanger Politics

Alice Gordon, Orange County Commissioner ◉

WE HAVE TWO PROBLEMS with this proposed acquisition: To participate in the wider vision, we agreed to put in $125,000 even though the acreage in Orange County appraised at half the $200,000 Durham is requesting. A government should not pay more than the appraised value for any property. Durham is disappointed with what we are offering. We had just been successful in securing eight acres adjacent to the Duke tract, but then it had never been offered to developers as this land has. Orange County has a working relationship with Duke University, and Duke calls us first when their land becomes available.

In 1997 I proposed the creation of the first comprehensive county land-acquisition program in North Carolina, now called the Orange County Lands Legacy Program. It covers the full spectrum of advice on protecting air and water quality and biological resources. Before this time everything went through the planning department. Now environmental protection is a separate department of Orange County with around five employees. For environmental reasons and the vision of completing the New Hope Corridor, we do not want this project to fail. I wrote the memorandum for the emergency meeting, the first to be held since I've been an elected official.

The Triangle Land Conservancy, the Pennys and Chapel Hill stepped in with $25,000 each, totaling the missing $75,000. We went into closed session. It was a long meeting partly due to one opposing person, but the remarkable thing is how fast this intergovernmental project is progressing. It usually takes years, not months.

Alice Gordon   11.5" x 3.5"   Oil on wood

Hollow Rock Creek   30" x 30"   Acrylic on wood

Wade & Carolyn Penny

WADE: JEFF FISHER HAD RECENTLY BOUGHT the old Hollow Rock store property and had already set-up his land with a conservation easement. Mid-December a meeting was called and we met again with Wendy, Ellen, Becky, Lisa, and a couple of others at the common house to discuss plausible options.

Carolyn: The developer had dropped off a plat plan. We wish we had known of the land's availability and had bought a strip. The plan provided no buffers to speak of.

W: The planning department's head rated the plan as exceptional, but it is an abomination to clear-cut a large mature forest, making way for their 3,000-square-foot houses with double garages. I grew up on a small lot with no trees. From the time I can remember—seven, eight, nine, ten years old—my mother would take us out to Randolph County, the family farm. That was like being in paradise; my brother and I would take off for three or four hours. All those beautiful hardwood trees, so much exploring to do. This area reminds me of that land of my childhood. Why did we move here? Because where we were was simply a city lot, and this is land.

C: At the January kick-off event, such a mix of people! It was very exciting. We bought 24 acres from Gertrude Rose in 1986 and had a contract to buy more whenever she wanted to sell. Protection of the land was understood. Both she and her husband (when he was alive) taught Sunday school. Mr. Rose would hook up his old white horse, Mandy, to the antique buggy and give rides around the main field. Mandy was never fenced; she followed Mr. Rose around like a dog. Mandy is buried in the Cathedral, the great field here surrounded by forest. Other horses, dogs, cats and the pets of good friends are

Wade & Carolyn
Oil on wood   12.5" x 6"

Mandy
30" x 30"   Oil on wood

also buried there. The developer's plan called for the development to come right up to the edge, completely violating the tranquility.

W: It can't happen. What we have here is a farm-house built around 1840, the old tool house, the woodshed, two bays built out of logs. Past the row of cedars sits the old barn, Mr. Rose's shop, the corn crib, tobacco barn, chicken coop. He had peacocks, guineas, you name it.

C: He'd take any animal given them. This land was to be protected. During this long arduous fight to protect the land, I know that the Roses have been with us, cheering us on.

W: I've got enough Scottish ancestry in me that I wasn't going to let an outside developer have the final say. My ancestors fought to keep the English out of the Scottish Highlands, and the fight's still there. This has been like a protracted high-stake's chess game. Someone had to do what Wendy did, organize, keep a unique, talented group on task. There has been lots of under-handed politicking happening, but we have very key individuals showing leadership. This has certainly been the thinnest margin of victory that I have ever witnessed.

Angela, Jeff and River
Oil on wood 12.25" x 6.5"

Jeff Fisher ● I ALWAYS KNEW I wanted to live here, preferably buy this portion. When I was in law school at UNC and at Duke for Environmental Resource Economics and Policy, I camped out here in a tent. Later I moved in with the occupants of the house above the Hollow Rock Store. There was lots of guitar playing and many elaborate practical jokes. The owner of the old store wanted to restore it, but things changed when the new bridge went in and he was denied permission to rebuild. I knew what this old cottage could become. When I bought the house with two acres, simultaneously the state bought from me public access rights, a conservation easement. Triangle Land Conservancy owns the adjacent land, so it would really work for them to underwrite this project.

Jeff & Angela's   9" x 9"   Oil on wood

Emily Eve Weinstein

I'd gone to meetings regarding the 100 acre tract, that is now being developed as Carillon, but I didn't get plugged in and highly involved until I realized the Duke Tract was on the development slate. At the first meeting I went about the fate of the Duke Tract, many were suggesting that our approach be to ask this current developer for greater buffers—50 to 70 feet. I didn't think that was acceptable. So I suggested, quite seriously, "Let's just buy it! Then we will have really BIG buffers! Let's just buy it outright!" People looked at me a little incredulously, but my enthusiasm caught on. At a city council meeting I was shot down by the city planner. He said it was a done deal, not even be thought about. I phoned Wendy from a coffee shop, "It's over." Wendy said, "No it isn't. Don't give up. We still have Becky, Ellen and Diane on our side! We can do this!"

At this point we attacked the development, but their plans were good compared to others, made better by their cluster housing and leaving natural areas. Our strategy now was to present *The Better Alternative* that would benefit the whole town. I talked with Wade Penny about the legal ramifications. He stated there was no guarantee they'd get water and sewer. The city planner tried to squash all hopes again by declaring it was already approved. We implored there MUST be a way. Finally he mentioned placing a four-month reservation on the land to figure out if it should become a park. Becky and Ellen scrambled to get it established, with a third vote coming from fellow commissioner Phil Cousin. However, the Durham open-space planner did not see this as a high priority; at this point she did not support our plan. But then nobody could ignore us when Wade and Carolyn stepped forward to more than double our preserved land.

When it looked like we were ultimately stumped again, this time by some of the Durham County Commissioners, I suggested a compromise: The county agrees contingent on the city coming through and Orange county raising their stakes $75,000. All this looked just unlikely enough so that when Ellen presented it they agreed. What they didn't count on is how much we wanted it. Triangle Land Conservancy, the Pennys, and their friend Bill Olive jumped in. Then there was that Orange County three-hour nail biter on the last day, the last hour of the reservation.

Looking back, EANG and the community effort to save this land is one of those things that I'll remember with my last breath as one of the reasons I was alive.

Secret Place...many know   6"x 6"x 2"   Acrylic – top of box

Lisa Cavanaugh ⊚ IT TOOK TWO ARTISTS SEEING what we didn't see to get the ball rolling. We learned a lot when we were unsuccessful in stopping the monster development nearby. Going to school, going to work, driving the car, the usual routine lulled us into complacency. The daily drill made us forget about the world around us. You and Alice woke me up, and then together we made our neighbors aware of what was at stake. When the magnitude became apparent, others readily jumped in, kind of like a relay race.

It's been a struggle for me, a Ph.D. student. More than anything I have wanted to dedicate my energy to this. It's not like any of us has extra time, but "I'm too busy" is NOT a valid excuse. How you spend your time is yours, of course, to decide, but some things have to take a back seat and some things can't. This is why our group effort has been so important, because when one couldn't, another could. It was important that we had a name and face, like Wendy, but just as important was the team effort.

What I feel best about is how we rallied the troops. Educating and raising awareness is the most exciting part of this. It really does take a village to raise a child, and it also takes a village to keep corporations, government, and society honest and aware. How could we not stand up for what we value, for the sentient beings that do not have a voice? How could we not? As Becky Heron says, "Once it's gone it's gone forever. God ain't makn' anymo' land."

Lisa and Lucky
Oil on wood 11.5" x 3.25"

Becky Heron, Durham county commissioner ⊚ YOU HAVE TO PLAY WATCH DOG all the time. I was one of the originals on the New Hope Creek Corridor Advisory Committee organized by the Mayor, Wib Gulley and Ken Coulter back in '91. Four jurisdictions paid in $10,000 each to do the master conservation plan. The Duke Tract we are looking at adding now will further protect the greenway. Adding in the Penny land it gives the opportunity to have a small park, a passive park with trails, connecting eventually to Jordan Lake.

Down the road, the Arrowhead Group worked to keep their land in the rural tier with low density. They had good reason with all their wetlands. Both developers and some landowners sought to turn it into suburban-zoned higher density. Zoning is good until someone wants to change it. Here, where I live, it was a dirt road. We were the only family with one other that wanted to keep it this way—dirt. We lost. All the rest couldn't see what a high-speed cut-through it would become. The Arrowhead Group has much to lose if zoning is changed.

The organization and dedication of the EANG reminds me of the first Eno River meeting. The city wanted to dam up a free-flowing river and make a reservoir! Nobody in this town knew the value of that river. We got recruited when my husband, Duncan and our son were out canoeing and a woman with very long hair called them over from the shore. This remarkable conservationist was Margaret Nygard, and from then on we were involved. Duncan made an Eno River slide show that every person in town saw. In 1976 the state started a folk festival, and by 1978 Margaret took it over; today it is known as the Eno River Festival. Through the entry fee, T-shirt sales, drink stands, booth fees, and membership dues, we raise our largest funds for buying more land.

That first year, Margaret got up on the stage and yelled, "It's a Miracle!" She got more accomplished on the federal, state and local level without getting anyone mad. What we are doing now is so reminiscent of then. When citizens get together and are singing off the same page out of the same book, we see what can get done. Officials will listen to citizens, then underwrite their efforts.

Becky & Rosie
Oil on wood
11" x 4"

Secret Place...many know   6" x 6"x 2"   Acrylic – inside of box

Mayor Bill Bell ◉

I'VE NEVER BEEN INVOLVED with anything so contentious... With the Little River Park we were to work with two municipalities, not an easy thing. The economics can be tricky. Now here with New Hope Creek Park, we have not two but four municipalities! All kinds of challenges will have been thrown into the mix. Will Durham County, I think, be able to get the grants needed? Managing the upkeep is not clear. Fortunately, the majority of it will be open space, a passive park.

It has become an easy call for me once we got past the money issue, particularly given the amount of land it now adds up to. My wife is constantly mentioning the transformation from a green landscape to cement everywhere. We want to maintain what we have, but balance encompasses a lot of elements, like our budget. We have many pressing things at this time. Acquiring park lands was not on anyone's radar. Our fiscal spending year starts the end of June, too late for this project. The window of opportunity would be gone. By February we have adopted the basic ideas. Cutting the city's share back to $75,000 makes it easier for me. It is highly unlikely we would have included the Duke Tract in the general budget, but more likely in a bond refer-endum for the voters to decide on in November as to whether to fund or not. It's in June that we make up our Christmas list. Who's going to benefit from it? What's it going to cost? And then we put it out to the public to vote on. Because of the time constraints, this park-land issue wasn't even discussed.

Hollow Rock Trail
12"x 4"   Oil on reclaimed wood

Mayor Bill Bell
Oil on wood 12.25" x 3.75"

Diane Catotti, Durham City Council member ⊚

WHAT PEOPLE WILL SAY PRIVATELY, versus what they'll commit to publicly, can vary greatly. Working to get this New Hope Creek Preserve added onto is a lot like how the Eno River Association started. So many last-minute changes, like folks switching votes. I was introduced to this request for land when Jeff approached me the day after election day, an already busy time. After a joint city/county meeting with the planning staff, Jeff, Wendy and myself laid out the map and reviewed how this could possibly be done. The development's cluster plan was good as far as these things go, but the water and sewer would be undergoing some long routing.

The argument against opposing the development is that it could be seen by the developer and his lawyer as arbitrary and capricious to not extend water and sewer lines. In Wake county the developers won a lawsuit we witnessed concerning just such a matter. We certainly did not want a repeat of that here. At a work session the head of planning, Frank Duke mentioned in passing that the county has the option to place a reservation, 120 days, to review all options. This was an "Ah-hah" moment! I said, "The county doesn't know that." Up to that point things were not looking good. We thought there was absolutely nothing we could do. Except now we learn it was a county option to place a reservation. So around 4 PM I stepped out of the meeting to call Ellen Reckhow on my cell phone. "Ellen, Frank Duke says the county has the opportunity to exercise an option to purchase the land and you have until 9 AM tomorrow morning to provide a letter of intent before it goes before the DRB." I stepped back into the meeting and announced, "A member of the County Commission has noted some interest in pursuing that option."

35

Emily Eve Weinstein

Diane with Ellie & Betsie   Oil on wood 11.25" x 6"

Emily Eve Weinstein

Cora Cole McFadden, Durham City Council member ◉

DURHAM OPEN SPACE AND TRAILS COMMITTEE oppose the purchase,
because funds are committed for the year. When it came before the city to
vote for the funds and support the project, I thought it was all lined up in
the affirmative, but there was this long pause. No one seconded Diane.
The mayor kept the motion open and alive, so she asked to speak to the
importance of the issue, but then Kevin Brice, with the Triangle Land
Conservancy, got up and offered the $25,000 from his organization.
We (Durham City) only had to pay $75,000 over three years. Hearing this,
I immediately seconded it. By making it very easy to pass, the project was
still alive. In the long run we win by preserving greenways. I just wish
the developer wasn't asking for so much in order to be bought out of
his contract.

Cora Cole McFadden
11.5" x 4"
Oil on wood

New Hope Stream
10" x 10"
Oil on reclaimed wood

Ellen Reckhow, Chair, Durham County Commission ◉ AT AROUND 4 PM I received a call from Diane Catotti, alarmed that Duke University is selling land along the New Hope for a subdivision. Since the property was outside the City limits, the County would need to take the lead. I decided to add it to our next agenda and ask the Board if they were willing to use a provision in the subdivision statute that allows us to reserve property for open space acquisition for a 120 day period. The reservation is placed and April 8 is our drop-dead date, whether we are going to go ahead and buy the land or not. At the Durham-Orange County work group meeting, I requested support from the other jurisdictions (Orange County, the City of Durham, and the Town of Chapel Hill) and put forward a possible funding proposal. Each government official there agreed to take it back to their Board.

Orange County was to pay $200,000, Chapel Hill $100,000, Durham city $100,000, and Jane Korest would be writing the land grants to fulfill Durham County's part of the $900,000. The remaining $200,000 is to be collected by citizen donations. The university made a mistake not offering it for park land in the first place, but then Duke's Tallman Trask possibly does one better by offering a three-year pay plan. This way we are able to tell each government they have three years. Coordinating the participation of four governments and other stakeholders is intense.

The key to this having a chance is that it is a great concept with enthusiastic support and tremendous lobbying effort by the Erwin Area Neighborhood Group. The tipping point is the Pennys' offer to sell the additional

Ellen Reckhow   11.5" x 3.25"   Cut-out, oil on wood

open space next to New Hope Creek at a rock bottom price, and their offer to donate a conservation easement on additional land they own. The combination gives critical mass to this project. The fact that other neighborhoods are adopting the cause, syndicating it, turns it into a cause the media can really roll with. The drama and intrigue are intense. My cell phone calls are greatly exceeding my allotted minutes!

When support from the City of Durham looked questionable, the Triangle Land Conservancy (TLC) offered $25,000 to defray part of the City's cost. When Orange County fell short by $75,000, the Pennys and TLC stepped up to fill that gap. TLC is filling a critical role in these last couple of weeks in helping to pull the whole funding piece together. We have met the April 8 deadline, and the commitment is being put in writing to buy the land from Duke over a three-year period. A great deal has been accomplished in 120 days! A special meeting is held and after two long hours we have approval of the revised agreement. Again, I look at my cell phone bill. This last week has been unbelievable. It's amazing I don't have an ulcer.

Hollow Rock Creek—Rock Wall
30" x 30"   Acrylic on wood

Reverend Phil Cousin ◉ THEY'VE ALL GONE DEVELOPMENT CRAZY. If folks see two trees standing together, they think that space needs to be developed. We are running out of open space, and greenways are extremely important. I want to hold onto the rustic element of this county, so when the farmland preservation projects come up, I support them. When I was first in office the proposal came up to have a landfill north of town, upstream from the Little River Reservoir. Well, *landfill*, as you know, is a nice word for *dump*! So we voted to buy that land and it became the Little River Park, but it could have been a disaster.

Being a county commissioner is another way for me to help people. I am the oldest of five sons; all five of us are third-generation clergy in the AME church. In this instance I was in the right place at the right time to assist. Many thought Duke's forest was development-proof even though there is no infrastructure to support it. But then a developer came along, and this was a neighborhood that assumed Duke Forest would be there forever, untouchable. That was just a presumption.

Reverend Phil Cousin
12.5" x 4.25"
Cut-out, oil on wood

Ancient Tree in Spring
8" x 8"
Oil on reclaimed wood

Randy Pickle ◉ THE SECRET AS TO HOW WE GREW to over 50 neighborhoods strong is the listserv. I received an email about the website committed to the Duke Tract, but couldn't access it. I contacted Wendy and offered web help. I've taken it over temporarily, also maintaining half a dozen others. Through the Inter-Neighborhood Council we are able to keep every area of Durham informed, thus quickly gaining support for the New Hope Creek Park concept!

Eno River Mural   6"x 6"x 2"   Acrylic – top of box

Randy Pickle   12" x 5"   Oil on wood

Eno River Mural   6"x 6"x 2"   Acrylic – inside of box

Kevin Brice, Executive Director of TLC

⊚ EACH OF THESE LAND PROJECTS turns into a catalyst.
40 acres expanding to over 100 is what makes it attractive to our board of directors. There are few straight-
forward projects. We kid ourselves, hoping this one will
be the exception and won't be difficult. Normally we of
the Triangle Land Conservancy

have to view it as too late when the landowners are
talking to developers, trying to sell for the maximum
amount. That gives us a clear picture that we are out of
the bidding. Normally we don't start at this late date in
a deal, but negotiate sooner with willing landowners.
The contention aspect is a new experience.

TLC's dealings in this area go back to the early eighties. The inventory taken then highlighted important natural spaces, but despite this we face a really tough project to go against, one already under contract to developers. And then The Deadline! Duke University's Talmon Trask, is a real friend of conservation, to have at this point even considered another option. The exit clause of paying off the developer $500,000 should Duke need to bail out came about after we got involved. The greatest single challenge, though, to closing this deal is the way it is playing out in the public arena in the newspapers and TV. There is just so much the media can do to capture the accuracy, the essence of the matter. It is difficult enough to close a deal in private and nearly impossible with the public eye shining so brightly on it. It has polarized folks, but it has also brought accountability. No place to hide! Perhaps this is another way to reach positive results.

Four years ago, Duke Forest manager Judd Edeburn contacted TLC about 1,000 acres in Chatham County for sale right along the Haw River. The trustees of Duke wanted to sell the land for fair market value, but they contacted us so that something could be done conservation wise. We talked with the Division of State Parks. The state purchased the land and soon the Haw River Slopes will open to the public. Once word got out, they were besieged by developers, and that is why it is so important that Duke first call TLC, Durham and Orange County. Confirmation of this policy is now being put into written form.

Kevin Brice   12" x 5"   Oil on wood

Stream   14" x 11"   Oil on reclaimed wood

Key Players   Cut-outs

Cora Cole
McFadden

Hildegard
Ryals

Becky
Heron

Alice
Gordon

Randy
Pickle

Ed
Harrison

Jane
Korest

Bill
Strom

Kevin
Brice

Mayor
Bill Bell

Mayor
Kevin Foy

Angela
Fisher

Jeff
Fisher

Group Portrait   Oil on wood

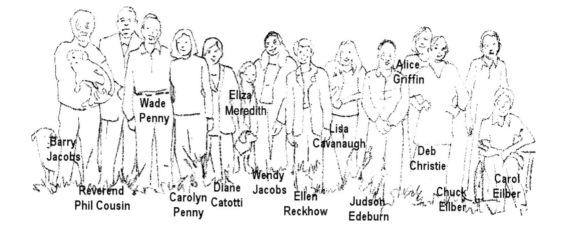

Portraits That Become Permanent Housemates ◆ THE CHAPEL HILL-

ORANGE COUNTY contingency was simply determined that all would go through. Every step of the way they have been magnificent except when it comes to returning my calls. I'm partially sad about this and partially okay. You see, these cutout figures of mine are a lot of work, and several of them I've done for this book will be living with me forever. I already have three never-bought portraits which I sneer at daily. I decide against doing anymore Lilliputian people when enthusiastic Ed Harrison phones. I've known of his activism forever. Okay, so one more portrait.

In the meantime, I'm taking a break by painting one of my cherished housemates. Fifteen years ago I adopted the handsome full-grown Casey from the Durham APS. He has moved several times with me and accepted all the other animals that have entered our lives. Cats turn a house into a home.

Casey on Chair   12" x 8"   Oil on wood

Kittens ◆ With all the frantic mess still going on about the land, I get e-mail after e-mail about animals in need. One situation sounds easy to solve and I do need a distraction. A family moved, leaving all their pets; foster homes are needed, and now. I hit reply, responding that I can take the two cats. My phone rings immediately. Only one cat is left, but she is very pregnant.

Blue Cream
8" x 8"
Oil on wood

After testing negative for communicable diseases, a scared basketball-shaped, long-haired tabby arrives at my place. She trusts no one, but hates it when I leave her alone. In the wee hours she delivers five scrawny kittens, one dead, another failing. The tuxedo kitten is loud when not clinging to the most engorged teat. After a few days it is clear they all have upper respiratory problems. My vet has me waiting in the lobby two hours, looks at them briefly and suggests I see how things play out. Two more die that night. I hire a new vet who makes house visits. All are put on antibiotics and within two days the remaining ones are thriving. Ms. Tux is the first to do everything. She climbs straight up, leaps long distances, is fearless. The blue-cream boy is demure and sweet. The Russian blue has a hole in her heart, possibly what took her siblings.

I leave for Europe in two weeks, and the fund raiser for the land happens this weekend! The foster felines will be here for another month. Fortunately, the pet-sitter will be here full-time. She is a vigilant animal caretaker. The dogs will go elsewhere so she can focus on kittens and cats. I will be both heartbroken and relieved when my foster cat family leaves.

Wilder   8" x 8"   Oil on wood

The Fundraiser: Art-for-the-Park

IN PUTTING OUR WALLETS WHERE OUR MOUTHS ARE, we need $50,000 more. I point out to Alice that the folks most active seem to be taking a breather. She has been sensing this also. We decide on an art fund-raiser from which 50% or more will go towards the purchase of the Duke Tract. I put together a paper invite to be distributed by hand. Granted, a mass mailing would be better, but heck, we need to raise the funds immediately. The event comes up in a week. I am panic-stricken. My friend and helper Anne comes over and we clean house, re-hang, group my art so we can fit in Alice's large watercolors and monoprints. Art instructor-naturalist Joe Liles prefers my studio to display his work. Yikes, now we need to clean that space, too, but it has to be done anyway as it hasn't been cleaned in a very long time. Joe plans to donate 100% of what he sells and is bringing a half dozen bottles of wine. We'll scrub the studio even if it means an all-nighter!

Alice and Wendy revise my announcement before I attempt to send it to 400 strong but my internet server shuts me down. Once reinstated, I finally e-mail it to all, in smaller groupings. Randy Pickle then sends it out to all his listservs. Not till the event itself will we know if anyone is coming. On the door of the room where kittens and cat reside, I have posted a sign proclaiming that they all need a home.

My boyfriend Marc, in Holland on a Fulbright, writes to apologize for not being here to help. We have only been together six months so I really do not know if his presence would be useful or not. He cooks well and has some organizational skills and bossy characteristics, like Anne, so probably it would have been good to have him present. Times like these I prefer that others make decisions. Maggie is printing greeting cards of Alice's art. Sally comes over with a huge array of knitted handbags, saying, "Price them as you want. I'm donating 100%." Vickie arrives with trays of food and buys four handbags. Kim Forehand donates ten of her *Coming Home* CDs. Deb Christie shows up with more food. Tina Motley will be bringing her clay sculptures. The doorbell keeps ringing and the dogs keep barking. Food and art continue to arrive. It will be the wee hours before I'm horizontal. It all starts at 2 PM tomorrow.

I did not know what to expect, so raising $3,000 in three hours seemed incredibly great, but then we hear that some inspired soul has donated $15,000! I'm exhausted. Lots of compliments about the house, which does look fantastic. I check on the kittens and then go to sleep.

Family Reunion   8" x 50"

Clyde's
12" x 14"
Oil on wood

Oil on reclaimed cedar siding

Shop Window   20" x 20"   Oil on wood

Reprieve ◆

ON OUR FIRST DATE MARC MENTIONED leaving for two months to teach at the University of Utrecht. I knew right then I'd be visiting Holland. Alice is very happy for me: "Why don't you go away? You are all edges. I hope you come back renewed." I promptly respond to Marc's invitation by asking which two consecutive weeks would work best. However, I find myself extraordinarily discombobulated upon landing in Europe for the first time in years. At least it's a milder sort of trouble than that with our New Hope Creek efforts.

Holland is perfectly flat and green. The air smells good and the water has no chlorine—impressive. And bikes outnumber cars twenty to one. It rains every day for a few minutes to a couple of hours. The plants benefit, and I am mesmerized by the hollyhocks growing from every sidewalk crack. I am hollyhock-crazy! It seems the whole country by its very existence honors the environment. Unfortunately, cobblestones are hateful annoyances when you're trying to get somewhere rolling a suitcase. Clunk, clunk, clunk. Also we go everywhere on Marc's clunker bike, me sitting sideways, smugly pleased to know my minor discomfort means I'm not carbon-dioxiding the atmosphere. Clunk, clunk, clunk. Marc thinks that riding double we look Dutch.

Animals are treated well here. Because I detest animal abuse, I have not gone back to Greece or Mexico and consider most of China off-limits, too. Holland's animals appear to be treasured. We are walking down a sidewalk when a cat that looks like Casey meows at me. He is staring at a black door. I knock on it. The door opens six inches and the cat scoots in. From within someone says, "Danka!" The door shuts. We rent a canoe to tour the canals and stop at an outdoor pancake restaurant where their pets reside beside the picnic tables behind a low wood fence: a goat, two sheep, a potbelly pig, and a cow with English setter markings. Such harmony delights me, and I recall our joy when our struggle back home finally means that we have saved some of what's right with the earth. As to cows, I wish I had the stomachs of one so I could finish more of my lunch,

Dutch Cat Like Casey   16" x 20"   Oil on wood

53

Emily Eve Weinstein

although Marc compliments me once again on my appetite.

The train takes us one hour south through farmland irrigated with carefully dug ditches; cows, sheep, goats range free. At our destination we walk from the train station to the theater where Marc and his fellow marine biologists will meet and network. We pass a wonderful dress-shop window, *The Goddess Within*. I insist on having a quick look. He suggests, "Checking this out alone will be much more fun for you. We can meet up in three hours at the theater." He leaves and I proceed to try on everything in the store. Ten minutes before our meeting time, I learn they do not take credit cards. I'm in shock: never have I done this kind of damage to my account for clothing, and the wispy stuff I'm buying weighs less than five ounces! On top of all this, I rush to the theater late. Marc is stunned that I have been in the one store the entire time, and even more amazed when I tell him how much I have to borrow from him. He looks at the small clump of lacy fabric and gushes, "You will look beautiful in that!" All my fear of buying flutters away and I try not to think of the car I bought for less or the tuition at the

The Outfit   14" x 10"   Oil on wood

Across the Street in Utrecht
16" x 12"   Oil on wood

state university I attended for the same amount. On the train back to Utrecht we look at the business card listing tarot reading, love potions, spells cast. I guess that's what happened to me!

We are to go next to Santiago de Compostela, Spain, for a conference. I have never gone to Spain because of bullfighting, though it is banned in Barcelona. Marc will be fully occupied with the conference. Our hotel is a long way from town so I take buses to art museums and then meet him at the exhibition hall. I try to learn something about marine sciences from the posters on display. Some of them would have served us well at city and county meetings on behalf of the New Hope Creek by illustrating run-off and mass-grading, two major environmental hazards. I also check out the complimentary pens and candy, but mostly I can't help

Around the Corner in Utrecht   14" x 20"   Oil on wood

comparing our New Hope Creek project to Marc's. While EANG is saving a creek and its land, he and his pals are trying to do the same with lakes and oceans!

With a crowd of scientists we visit an ornate cathedral. Written especially for the conference attendees, the sermon lauds their roles as caretakers of our great planet. I feel the words are meant, too, for us who have worked so hard back home to save a bit of our world.

Fragrant incense and an angelic voice fill the chapel. I look for the owner of the remarkable voice as it softly recedes and see a somberly dressed nun move forward to take another Sister's place and continue their haunting song. The nun's move like gentle gray mice.

Liz and Ron's New Home and Garden   14" x 16"   Oil on wood

Back Home, Visiting at the Rose Homestead ◆ LIZ AND RON MOVED THEMSELVES and their plants about 18 months ago to another equally ancient residence on a dirt road. This one has traffic, soccer moms and construction workers from the monster development taking a short-cut. Thus the garden beds only ramble on three sides because the dust thrown during dry weather coats the plants. The traffic has been something to get used to.

On the positive side, Liz has a studio here and is painting more than she has in years. They still feel the presence of the horse, Mandy. Her large white body was once seen crossing the road on a foggy morning, disappearing into the woods. A middle-aged local recounted this to Liz. At the time of the sighting, the local was a small boy going fishing.

A Familiar Face ◈ ED HARRISON REMINDS ME how back in the spring of 1984 along 15-501 many acres of natural forestation were bulldozed to make way for yet another strip mall. We got to watch as redbuds, dogwoods in full bloom, new fresh growth on all the trees were pushed down, smashed up, run over, and for the final insult, burned in huge mangled piles. Ed recounts the brutality of this waste of life at the height of growth. Around this time Becky Heron partnered with Hildegard Ryals to start the county-wide preservation campaign, with the first local focus on New Hope Creek. Then in 1989-90 they formed the visionary New Hope Creek Advisory Committee with Ken Coulter and Duke professor Bob Healy to put some protection in place. At that time, there was none to speak of. Ed was then hired by Triangle Land Conservancy as their biologist and plant ecologist. He put out the word that all species needed to be inventoried. Volunteer Liz Pullman hiked between Hollow Rock and the Leigh Farm for years, listing all flora and fauna. Ed likes to explain how our passive park is in keeping with over 20 years of thinking...

(See Appendix **B,** page 80 for a continuation.)

Ed Harrison
Cut-out
Oil on wood 12" x 4.5"

57

Emily Eve Weinstein

The Cathedral, the field in front of Mandy's grave and the final resting place of all of the animal companions of Gertrude and Bernice Rose.

9.5" x 11.5"   Oil on wood

Elect Like-Minded Officials ❖ Chapel Hill's Mayor Kevin Foy's number one suggestion to me is to "Elect like-minded officials."

Chapel Hill is the pretty little town to our west. South, north and west they have rolling hills, forests and greenways. To their east is Durham. The sprawl of strip malls, old shopping centers and brand new ones litter business highway 15-501 between Chapel Hill and Durham. Mayor Foy has declared that citizens above all must elect people who are already committed to the environment. "This is fundamental to maintaining reasonable growth," he says. "All nine members of our elected council stressed environmental commitment in their campaign and look for opportunities to protect land. In 1984 Chapel Hill effectively drew a boundary around itself: the town made the environmentally enlightened decision not to sprawl. Add to that, Orange County employs a full-time land conservationist who looks for land to save."

Chapel Hill, out of the four jurisdictions, was the first to make a financial commitment. No massive letter campaigns or arm twisting was needed. Mayor Foy and his green-minded council made their independent decision to back the New Hope Creek project as it unfolded, took a broader long-range view of the needs of our unique region, and then worked to convince Durham City, Durham County and Orange County to commit also.

Durham is at least double the size of its neighbor and is combating a gang and drug problem head-on, making positive inroads. It is now time for Durham to take steps to preserve our rich history and our abundant natural resources. Sprawl goes unchecked when a city's sewer and water is allowed to arbitrarily be over-developed out into the countryside. Such would stretch Durham to the limit. Chapel Hill's Mayor Foy explains that they managed to put a cap on this by not extending water and sewer lines beyond their city's limit.

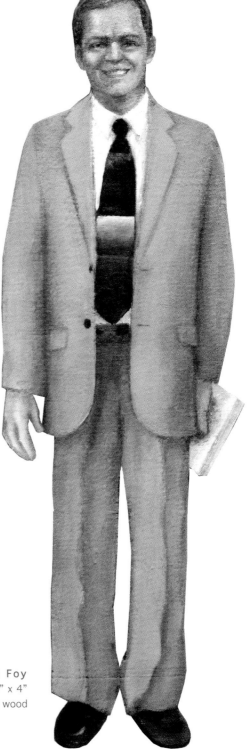

Mayor Kevin Foy
12.5" x 4"
Cut-out, oil on wood

The Cathedral,
seen through fall
leaves
9" x 7.5"
Oil on wood

A Like-Minded Elected Official ◆ EANG SPOKESPERSON AND

occasionally my conscience, Wendy, repeats that Chapel Hill's mayor pro tempore is about to become even more key to the New Hope Creek Park. Bill Strom is on the newly formed park's task force representing Chapel Hill in an elected capacity, and he takes his role seriously: "There is a great deal of work ahead of us. We must carefully create, through a transparent public process, a vision for the park that lives up to everyone's expectations."

During part of the time I was trying to track down the Orange County-Chapel Hill contingent, Mr. Strom and his wife Jennifer were hard at work in Katrina-devastated Mississippi, where, as Strom explained, the entire infrastructure of towns like Waveland and Pass Christian, Louisiana, where they and others labored, has been destroyed. Jennifer, a former board member of Independent Animal Rescue, used a network her group had in place to help the affected animal population. On the Bayou Rescue website, the Stroms' work and that of others were reported on daily. So now I know of Chapel Hill's mayor pro tem both through his work in the Bayou and his clear voice for environmental and social concerns.

What I did not know was Strom's affective hidden efforts. "The focus of Durham's mayor, Bill Bell, was elsewhere," he said. "I phoned him multiple times explaining that this was a short-term opportunity and urged him to back it. It was the same with all three of the other jurisdictions because there is a lot of scrutiny given when we walk outside the expected lines, and this would be an atypical collaboration. Government is not nimble. It moves slowly. Behind the scenes there was much arm twisting." Thankfully, Chapel Hill elected environmentally minded officials who negotiated behind both closed and open doors for the land.

Within the region, Strom knows many of the elected officials and worked closely with them on the Land Legacy Program and more recently the FREE transit system. Within this small town you can now be dropped off within walking distance to everywhere. Orange County sometimes forgets that this progressive town is within its boundaries. Strom and his associates had a breezy time backing the New Hope Creek

Bill Strom   12.25" x 4.25"   Oil on wood

Emily Eve Weinstein

project, but then bringing in Orange County was much
harder because of one holdout, Moses Carey, the chair.
Carey disagreed strongly with fellow county commissioners Alice Gordon and Barry Jacobs, and he also was in
opposition to the city of Chapel Hill. I will never forget
the two-hour wait as they negotiated behind closed
doors. The positive thing about the opposition is that
their forcing us to organize our arguments made us
stronger and louder on behalf of the land.

As Chapel Hill's mayor pro tem says, "When citizens
partner with conservation groups and government, the
possibilities are endless. This has been a remarkable
collaboration."

New Leaves
8" x 8"
Oil on wood

Catching Up With Deb ❖ YES, WE HAVE BEEN SUCCESSFUL, but many participants are still reeling in the wake. Deb's portrait cutout was one of the first to be done and we have spoken several times since, but not about this whole ordeal, which turned out so well. The New Hope Creek Preserve, purchased by four jurisdictions, is now the future spearhead of the trail system.

Deb worked alongside Alice and me painting signs, posting them, making AstroTurf pins, attending meetings, despite being involved in building a house. With her legal background she asked astute questions, helping matters take a positive course. She also compiled our pledger database, having recognized that the growing pile of scraps of paper were bound to get lost. The database then went to our supporting non-profit, Triangle Land Conservancy, who collected contributions ranging from $5 to $15,000.

(See Appendix **C,** page 81 for a continuation.)

Deborah Christie
Cut-out
Oil on wood 12" x 5"

Roots   5" x 8"   Oil on salvaged wood

Putting the Pieces Together ◆ A GIGANTIC QUESTION
HAS NOT been answered up to now: How does a project
get funded? Over a million dollars is needed in our case.
We the people have managed to bring in a little over
$200,000; our backer, the nonprofit Triangle Land
Conservancy, has kicked in $50,000, $25,000 going
towards Orange County's part and the Pennys contribute
$25,000 as well. Four jurisdictions have finally voted for
the purchase, and their contributions total almost
$1,225,000. At this point, after all the

meetings, coaxing, bullying, hair-pulling, speeches, fund-
raising, and near death of it all, the final, boring and
tedious phase rests with Jane Korest, the Open Space
and Real Estate Manager for Durham County, whose job
is to now find major grant sources to make this project
affordable. Some of the most active EANG members
didn't even know of her, what she does, or her key position. I'm embarrassed to admit that I am one of those.

Jane gets three or four calls a year to write major

Wood Beetle　　10" x 10"　　Oil on wood

Jane Korest
Cut-out
Oil on wood 12" x 3.5"

land grants. An autonomous agent she is not; until it's a board project, on the plan, she can't go gung-ho. What she can do is step forward with her evaluation, declaring the project a priority while still balancing the needs of the board. During this process emotions can run very high. She has had more than a few developers mad at her. I asked Jane if she worked in tandem with Triangle Land Conservancy. She responded by reciting the director's phone number and extension.

(See Appendix **D,** page 82 for a continuation.)

The Hanging Rock   5" x 5"   Oil on salvaged wood

Painting by Moonlight Along Bolin Creek ❖

WITH NEARLY A FULL MOON and a clear night, I must go paint. Marc suggests Bolin Creek Park, Chapel Hill's greenway. Marc adds that I absolutely must take the dogs, and Kali and China agree that they need an adventure. China, the larger, is always ready to provide more protection than is needed, so Marc agrees to take her for a spin as I work with the less intense Kali by my side. Plan in place, we drive to the park. The winding pedestrian road with billowing trees makes for perfect subject matter. Heading out on the path, we ignore an entwined couple the dogs flush out. Ambling along the creek at a bend in the road, we see that the moonlight clearly displays a variety of tall old-growth oaks, undergrowth and flowering wild bushes. Up ahead a steep path to the right leads to the Café Driad. Tonight folk rock drifts through the thick forest. Marc aims in the music's direction, canine companion close by his side. Kali settles in beside me as I turn my five gallon plastic paint kit upside down and prepare to paint.

Less than a quarter mile away from where I sit is bustling Chapel Hill. When the University is in full session, this quaint town explodes with pedestrians and traffic. As the University grows, so does the need for a way out of the congestion. With each passing year the greenway's importance becomes

Emily Eve Weinstein

Bolin Creek Trail   14" x 10"   Oil on wood

more obvious, a tranquil place that helps keep the area livable. Here, too, there is a group called Friends of Bolin Creek championing the continued health and existence of the park. They have succeeded in getting Carrboro, Orange County, the University, and the Orange County Water and Sewer Authority on board.

The small town next door, Carrboro, now needs to take up the lead in continuing to develop the greenway. Our hope is they will be able to preserve, ridge to ridge, a wider corridor. The University has been a benign landlord, but hesitant to commit in perpetuity to the environmental protection of the land because of potential expansion needs. The woods surrounding Bolin Creek are a significant source of pleasure; they are, for example, honeycombed with bike trails substantial enough to be written up in national mountain-bike magazines.

A dog strolls by grumbling, with person close behind. Kali growls, I tell her to stop, she does. The two strangers continue past, but for a long stretch I hear the dog mumbling obscenities and complaints as they disappear into the dark. Obviously, earlier, farther up the trail, the dog must have met China. The painting complete, Marc and my guard dog appear. "She bumped into a dog off-lead and really surprised him," he said. I told Marc I had suspected as much.

China and Kali   12" x 8"   Graphite on paper

Rails-to-Trails Path   14" x 16"   Oil on wood

Rails-to-Trails ◆ WE ARE PAINTING THIS THURSDAY morning south of town, Alice with her watercolor setup, me with my grungy oil-painting bucket. This segment of trail is part of Durham's Park and Recreation Department. The Rails-to-Trails Conservancy has adopted many abandoned railroad lines across the United States, converting them into wheelchair accessible, automobile-free terrain for hiking, biking, skating, and horseback riding. This is the largest trails organization in the nation, boasting over 100,000 members committed to maintaining and developing this extensive trail system. In Durham it is known as the American Tobacco Trail, which reflects the historical primary use here of the railroad.

Apex Bridge Closed ◈

DIANE IS MEETING ME at the Apex Street Bridge, another access point of the Triangle's Rail-to-Trail system. A pedestrian bridge goes over the path, a road now closed to traffic as it was deemed unsafe for heavy vehicles. It could have been torn down or rebuilt, and some see closing it as racially motivated, as was also stated by some during the placement of Durham's train lines and the expressway. I suspect it was more a matter of economics. As I stand on the bridge and look across to the white-collar section and then to the blue, I see that half the residents take care of their property, the other half don't.

Diane has stayed up above on the bridge under full shade with her fancy portable easel. I opt for a more dramatic view with less cover; in other words, I move with the transitory shadows to avoid frying. Finally giving up, I begin throwing all my supplies back into my five-gallon container when a walker asks to see my painting. When I tell her it may be in a book on land conservation, she lights up. She has recently moved here from Miami, where with a group of fellow activists they put through a bond referendum for $90,000,000 to go towards purchasing environmentally endangered land. Specifically,

Mimosa with Five Birds
8" x 10"   Oil on wood

she worked on a parcel that was little more than an acre, one of the few natural areas in a densely populated city, which went for $1,000,000. The Miami environmental planner for this case turns out to have been my best high-school friend in Islip, New York. What a small world we live in! It helps dramatize how saving our magic places is so very crucial.

Apex Street Bridge   14" x 10"   Oil on wood

This part of the trail goes on for eight miles. The steep walls are covered in kudzu and wisteria. All these hikers, bikers, joggers make me feel guilty for doing none of these things. I lug my half-melted self up the ramp to Diane, still happily painting in full shade. Her subject is not as dramatic as mine, but she has been able to take it further with texture, rich darks and lights. After all, she hasn't spent the time dodging the sun's rays.

Another Development ◆ UP THE ROAD FROM the New Hope Creek, the Arrowhead Group neighborhood meeting is being held at the elementary school. I watch as the developer's rep evades questions. He shares no information. He is here to let the residents vent and attempt to assess how difficult the resistance is going to be to their proposed development. The slick bamboozler from months past relished his role as a blowhard. He may be OK for this kind of meeting, but I sense they'll be sending bigger guns to the County Commissioner's meeting.

Sure enough, Mr. Big Gun, their lawyer, is ever present at the public hearing, threatening a lawsuit. He argues that they have followed the rules and regulations completely; they are within the zoning laws; nothing should block their way. On paper, he tells the truth, but in reality this neighborhood has much to fear. After more than two years of fighting developers who want to do an end run around the 2030 Comprehensive Plan (which placed Arrowhead in the Rural Tier over two years ago so that its rural character would be 'protected'), it is clear that

Private Road   6.5" x 8"   Oil on board

Arrowhead residents, the County Commissioners and Planning Department officials do not want the developer to be able to proceed with his high density/environmentally insensitive plan. But, as unbelievable as it seems, they are all stymied by laws and technicalities which favor the developer. There might be room for 40 houses on the 91 acres, but certainly not 97. The residents have authentic concerns, such as wells drying up and their water sources being polluted by run-off. Back in 1989, a developer came in and discovered most of the land doesn't perc making it unsuitable for such a level of development, but not before his bulldozer obliterated all in its path, including a large outcropping of rocks. The boulders were nowhere to be found!

If this next round of developers are allowed to disturb the ecological balance, they will discover the impossibility of building enough houses to justify their cost. The unwillingness to work with the Arrowhead Group's concerns is a serious problem. Once allowed to proceed they will be no better than the monsters around the corner. On one entrance to the proposed development, a blind bend in the road where they plan to pave an entrance would involve a turn lane potentially jeopardizing one of Durham's largest trees. At the other entrance, two 50-year-old ponds that support a multitude of fish and bird life will be drained, filled and replaced with concrete. The Arrowhead Group has fought to keep the area intact for the past three years, going so far as to get the area re-zoned rural from residential. If the developers had been willing to cooperate with the land instead of combatting it, this community would have worked with them.

Saving Magic Places

OIL ON RECYCLED CANVAS   4.5' x 3'

A COUPLE YEARS PRIOR to the concept of this book, Noelle Paule phoned me, "Can you use a large canvas? My sister Wicca, did a huge portrait of me. It's nice but I'm tired of living with BIG me."

The canvas is 4 by 3 feet; Noelle's massive curly red hair is featured in full. I have no idea what I will do with this interesting painting—I certainly will not gesso over it. Three years later I'm told of a massive tree in jeopardy due to reckless developers. To draw attention to its magnificence I decide to set up my easel by the great tree.

The largest canvas in my studio was this donated painting. It became eerily clear why it landed here: to protect the tree everlasting. Thank you, Wicca Davidson for painting the first layers and thank you Noelle for your generosity in donating it and for all you do for animals.

Emily Eve Weinstein

Unlike Arrowhead, down the road we were in a unique position to get public support as the forest we fought to protect was connected to a greenway and other publicly accessible land. Here we have a thick forest with a beautiful winding stream on private property. A couple falls ago I saw that the most magnificent vista would be from atop that hill, part of the land that the Arrowhead Group is protecting. With art supplies in tow I asked permission to set-up. I was told a flat "no". No trespassing, didn't I see the signs? So mildly put, significant support from outside groups is not going to happen. But it doesn't matter if I'm never allowed to paint from that sought-after vantage point. It supports thousands of birds, mammals, reptiles, insects and a clear stream. Those are enough reasons for me, but maybe the dangerous entry, lack of suitable soils and terrain for perc sites, lack of available well sites, poisonous run-off, and ecologically insensitive site plans will be enough to shut down the proposed development in Arrowhead.

Two Moon Pond
9" x 8.5"
Oil on salvaged wood

The Quarry   10" x 14"   Oil on wood

Quardian of the Quarry ❖ IN 1982, HAVING JUST ARRIVED in Durham, I went with a new friend to the local swimming hole. We parked in a sanctioned Eno River State Park parking lot, then walked on a path that squiggled through the woods, straight down a hill, over an embankment, and through a rocky stream. Finally we found ourselves gazing across a four-acre hidden jewel, a lake where, I later learned, most who visited went skinny dipping.

I once invited a fellow I dated, Ron, to go there with me. He loved the serenity of the place and imagined living there. Eventually we stopped seeing each other. We moved at incompatible speeds; Ron was country, I was still very city. I continued to hike and swim at the

Quarry, but the place was becoming progressively packed, and litter was everywhere. The last time I went I spied three men with large prison tattoos, a tarp strung between trees and a bonfire blasting. I retreated fast, unnoticed, never imagining I'd ever go back.

Several years passed and Ron phoned. I was delighted. He invited me to see where he now lived. I drove down Route 70 to a small access road and turned as instructed onto a long dirt driveway with only two houses, the small cottage Ron rented and the ranch house his elderly landlady lived in. After we caught up on our lives, my long-lost friend told me he had to show me something. We walked outside and down the dirt drive, past his house and about a quarter of a mile into the woods, across a field, down an embankment, when all of a sudden there was the Quarry! Ron had answered an ad to rent a small house, the closest human residence to this lake. His landlady, Margaret Coile, was frustrated and saddened by the state of things. Ron sympathized deeply with her concerns and made it his other job to clean up the mess, forcing trespassers to leave. He carried an official looking walkie-talkie which he used whenever he spotted an unwelcome guest, who would then be intercepted by a police-man or a park ranger. Ron also carried out over 100 large black plastic bags of litter. The place, unoccupied except for us, was now pristine. Ron had saved the Quarry.

I mentioned to a friend how the Quarry had been resurrected. She said everyone knew it was now too dangerous to visit. A mad-man with a shotgun patrolled the place, she said, "and he might shoot you."

Trail to the Quarry
16" x 12"   Oil on salvaged wood

Emily Eve Weinstein

I thought she was more than a little crazy passing on such a nutty rumor. The second time I went to visit Ron and his private swimming hole he picked up a rifle to take along. I was shocked. I asked, "Uh, isn't that overkill?" No, he claimed he'd been threatened many times, and besides people were slobs and there were no exceptions to be made. A father and son hiked in just in time to bump into us. Ron stopped them. In a voice straight out of the film *Deliverance*, he tells them to turn around and retreat fast. Didn't they read all the signs? They are on private property he says as he phones his buddies at headquarters. They leave. I ask him if he wasn't just a little harsh. "No, not at all," he replies. We walk back in the direction of these most recent trespassers, and sure enough, we spot a gum wrapper and a burning cigarette.

Three years after Ms. Coile died, Ron returned to Texas at the coaxing of his ex-wife. After he departed, the place remained free of people for years as the tales of the gun-toting vigilante patrolling the place continued. In actuality, the Eno River State Park has acquired all 159 acres and it is now open to the public. Rangers helping at the parking lot make sure all are gone by 8:30 PM, tickets are written for littering, dogs must be leashed. I asked a ranger if he knew Ron. "Oh, yeah, we liked him. When the place was off-limits, he made our job easy. People would come out into the parking lot and tell us they were shot at. We'd tell them "If he'd wanted to shoot you he would have. One run-in and they'd never come back!"

Slowly a quieter crowd is returning with bathing suits and inner tubes. "Hopefully with a little more respect," Ron told me over the phone after I described the transformation to him.

Quarry Defender
10" x 4"
Graphite on paper

Update ◆ TWO YEARS AFTER THE STRUGGLE began to save this land, Wendy tells me that although we have been successful, finally the papers have just been signed. The land is slated to become a passive park, but we can also see how items tied up in government tend to move slowly when no one is pushing.

Just after the victory Wendy journaled: "...and all this with the clock ticking. The countdown began on December 8, 2004, when Durham County invoked their right to a 120-day reservation on the Duke land to evaluate its importance to the public interest. Thus a deadline loomed, April, 8, 2005, when a contract with Duke University was due in hand. It's hard enough to navigate the rules, procedures, agendas, schedules, work sessions, committee meetings, public hearings, personalities, and politics of one government. But four jurisdictions at the same time?

"It was a Sisyphean struggle. Each time we had a victory, took a step forward, got that boulder closer to the top, we would hit the next obstacle to overcome, and the boulder would roll partway down again. But we all held each other up. Every phone call, every e-mail, every bumper sticker, every yard sign, every financial pledge, every appearance at a meeting, every petition, every visit to our website, every newspaper article, every letter to the editor, every editorial, every event, every endorsement from a

Down the Road   9" x 7"   Oil on wood

neighborhood group helped push that boulder up the hill. And none of us ever let go at the same time. We each had our moments of doubt or exhaustion, but there would always be someone with optimism, energy, and new ideas to pull us all together and help us devise a new way to lever that boulder along.

"We had faith that ordinary people can make a difference. Faith that our government officials would hear us and advocate for our best interests. Faith that human beings can speak for those who have no voice—the water, the trees, the creatures of the forest, just like Dr. Seuss's Lorax.

"Perhaps it's just as my husband Michael says, that all of the planets were aligned in the right place, at the right time. The four planets of our four local governments, each with their own stars, like Ellen, Becky, Phil, Diane, Barry, Alice Gordon, Bill, Kevin, and Ed, and their planetary forces, created favorable conditions and helped guide us in making the right decisions. Then there was that swirling cosmos of stars, the hundreds of people from neighborhoods all across Durham and Orange, whose actions, big and small, created a groundswell of support for taking a risk and seizing the moment to make New Hope Creek Park Preserve happen. Then there were those special stars, people like Lisa, Jeff and Deb, who had the vision and light to help lead the way. And the guardian angels, the Pennys and Kevin and TLC, standing quietly in the wings, but always there to step forward, keep us moving, and really causing things to happen."

Primarily doing the art side of the work, I was still buffeted from the grueling ping-pong politics of it all, but I never doubted victory because imagining the opposite would have been too painful. And then, all of us, myself included, our helpers and thousands of backers working together, those that did the politicking, the hand-to-hand negotiating, even while feeling ulcers forming, felt exuberant. I do believe success requires that you visualize your goals as already realized, demand that the outcome be nothing less than those goals, and know deeply that success must include all those involved, each and every one, doing whatever they can to the very best of their abilities.

Clothesline   14" x 16"   Oil on salvaged wood

May all your magic places live unto eternity!

New Hope Creek   18" x 24"   Oil on canvas

A

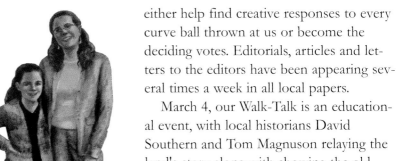

Wendy Jacobs (cont'd. from page 22) - The fact is, that the Duke land was supposed to be for open space and recreation and that we needed the Duke Tract as an urban gateway into the New Hope Creek Corridor and to further protect New Hope Creek watershed. Hence, we make the case for completing the New Hope Creek Master Plan. Just prior to the BIG night Maggie creates our website with mission statement while Rick sets up the listserv, which Don Weil starts adding names to and Lisa and Taymon continue doing so. Community activist Randy Pickle offers to take over the website, and Kevin McPeak, whom to this day I have never laid eyes on, e-mails with the offer to set-up an on-line pledge form. This really makes it easy for folks to pledge their donation, in seconds! The listserv, which goes to the entire neighborhood, environmental groups, political and personal listservs makes it possible to enlist hundreds for action alerts.

Between our huge kick-off event and the next one, March 4, we are working at our goal of raising $100,000. Our other focus is to get the four legs of government on board—Durham City and County, Orange County, and Chapel Hill. Every single meeting we attend we either dress in green or wear our astroturf pins or both. Sometimes only a couple show up, but occasionally as many as twenty attend. At each leg of government we have a guardian angel, a supporter, an official who values the importance of open space preservation. Angel county commissioner Ellen Reckhow develops a plan involving all four goals and how much they need to contribute. Ellen and the other key guardian-angel officials, Becky Heron, Diane Catotti, Bill Strom, Ed Harrison, Barry Jacobs, Kevin Foy, Phil Cousin and Alice Gordon

either help find creative responses to every curve ball thrown at us or become the deciding votes. Editorials, articles and letters to the editors have been appearing several times a week in all local papers.

March 4, our Walk-Talk is an educational event, with local historians David Southern and Tom Magnuson relaying the land's story along with showing the old colonial road and providing a physical tour of the tributaries. Reporters and 80 supporters are present. All this with only ten well-posted signs and the almighty listserv. It is raining, pouring, in fact. We cluster together figuring what to do next, when the sun bursts through; umbrellas are closed, raincoats come off, and away we trek! At this time we have 40 neighborhoods on board. Even the most opposed couldn't say this project wasn't for the entire community. March 4 is also exactly one month from D-day (do or die), when the 120-day reservation runs out. Our backing environmental group, Triangle Land Conservancy, puts our challenge up to $150,000. TLC becomes active when the Pennys commit to donate a 37-acre conservation easement as well as a bargain sale of 25 acres, increasing the puzzle piece now to 106 acres. Of course, our letters to the editors, letters to Duke, e-mails to elected officials, and face-to-face meetings continue.

Chapel Hill gets the ball rolling: on March 24 they vote unanimously to contribute their $100,000 portion of the creation of New Hope Creek Park. Now it is Durham County's turn. The developers employ a powerful lawyer known for working on behalf of developers. Soon after, the campaign is threatened with an editorial that is full of misleading information. At the County Commissioner meeting, I respond to the lies very forcefully. Durham County goes into closed session and we wait and wait...two hours. We wait for the verdict. It is life or death. Becky Heron and Ellen Reckhow we know will vote for the park. Phil Cousin comes through, but his "yes" vote is contingent on Orange County providing the $200,000, which would be $75,000 more. Where and how are we going to do this?

On the same day in the evening is the Durham City Council meeting. This turns out to be our worst nail-biting experience as the city struggles to refuse our pleas. There are many other pressing needs in this city, and the value of preserving open space is lost on them. They vote, we lose by one. Within one minute six months of work is gone, dead, done, we die. Suddenly Cora Cole-McFadden realizes she was confused by the wording and cast her vote the wrong way. A recount is called. This time we win by one vote! We are back to life. The important thing is that we do not give up.

The next day desperate to raise $75,000 in two days, we go back to the Chapel Hill Town Council asking them to help us get over the finish line. They come through with an additional $25,000, as well as TLC and the Pennys!

The following day, the day before Durham County must sign the contract with Duke for the land, the Orange County Commissioners hold an emergency meeting and go into a closed session. It is now all up to them...the stakes are high, it's all four governments on board, or nothing.

A Familiar Face (cont'd. from page 57) - Chapel Hill was the first jurisdiction to commit to New Hope Creek Park, so their town council member, Ed, along with the rest of the Chapel Hill crew, attended the meetings of the three other constituencies. With their Green AstroTurf pins prominently displayed on lapels, they are seated to stare down the three remaining votes. I'm reminded how important all the Orange County players are, absolutely crucial, but I could be creating my cutouts for the rest of eternity. Ed recounts how during the first Durham City Council work session on this park Becky's cell phone rang continuously: Ellen Reckhow was locked outside City Hall. She needed to find out more about the 120-day reservation that could be set into motion. She just heard from Diane Catotti with this news.

Ed was not at the legislative tour as he and wife Pat were hiking in the Smokies. It didn't seem imperative that he be there as all key factors seemed to be in place, although there were still many missing pieces to the greenway. From my place Ed headed over to the New Hope Advisory Committee meeting. The big topic would be connecting Brown Wetlands and Wood Lots. This land is slated for a perpetual environmental easement, never to be developed, but rather restored to its prior grace before settlers and slaves dug trenches and berms. Having followed Ed over to this meeting, I recognized Bob Healy of Duke, Bill Olive (major donor to EANG) and Jon Kent of New Hope Stream Watch, to name only three. All of them, and many more, have been integral to the success of the new park.

Back when EANG was just heating up, Ed pulled out his old Duke Forest map, a piece of paper 34 years old displaying all the tracts of forest, individual parcels viewed by the university as laboratories and outdoor classrooms, each numbered. Classroom Number One almost became a development, and now it is the New Hope Creek Park!

❧ Appendix ❧
C

Catching Up With Deb (cont'd. from page 63) - Deb's database proved essential, since Ellen Reckhow several times increased the fund-raising goal from $100,000 to $150,000 to $200,000, with the list of pledgers eventually growing to over 300! Every aspect of this campaign has run on individual incentive. For instance, a committee led by Susan MacKinnon came up with the brochure; Alice, Joe Liles and I put together Art-for-the-Park; Jon and Bea Miller held a plant sale; Sandy and Mike Bisdee organized a dance concert of rock n' roll to raise funds; Wendy connected all the dots; and so on it went.

In this spirit of helping to pull all the pieces together, Bill Holman, director of the Clean Water Management Trust Fund, proposed a legislative tour to improve our chances of getting the CWMTF grant. What with Wendy exhausted, Jeff changing jobs, Alice weakened from her cancer treatment, and Lisa back in school, we had an organizational vacuum. It did not seem that we had anyone to orchestrate such an event, which would take enormous logistical preparation—definitely NOT "my thing." The legislative tour is pivotal to the grant Jane Korest is writing for $1,000,000 towards this project. Yet despite the whirlwind which is Deb's life, she steps in and produces a flawless event.

On a hot but beautiful Monday morning, July 25, Jane Korest, Jeff Masten and Rich Shaw lead North Carolina legislators, local governmental officials, and staff of the CWMTF along paths in the New Hope Creek Lands, said paths prepared by the hard work of Jeff, Judd Edeburn, Rich Shaw, Mike Giles and Phil Leinbach. Hildegard provides popsicles. *The Herald-Sun* sends a photographer. The next day, featured, is a four-column photo of Bill Holman looking over "Hanging Rock" at New Hope Creek as well as a smaller image of a group of children welcoming the guests with individual painted signs, each stating "THANK YOU!" to Duke, Triangle Land Conservancy, Durham County, City of Durham, Orange County, and Chapel Hill. The 6 o'clock news covers the event that night on our local WTVD-11, with television news featuring interviews with Wade, Wendy and Becky. The event attracts lots of publicity for the CWMFT and the New Hope Creek Preserve. The North Carolina Legislature had not committed enviromental funds elsewhere, but several weeks after the tour full funding for the CWMTF was granted in the general budget.

D

Putting the Pieces Together (cont'd. from page 65) - Once the obvious obstacles are cleared, Jane Korest then takes on the project as her own special mission because she wants every one of her proposals to be a winner. She understands on a personal level the pain that comes with losing open spaces. As she has said, "As a child I remember the fields with bunnies ending up with houses on top of them." Her job is to get the money to help make

protecting open space affordable for Durham County. It takes real dedication to write compelling in-depth grants, each generally around 24 pages, what with narrative, supplemental questions, maps and budgets, layers of policy, all vast. She has to be a combination botanist, mathematician, wordsmith.

Part of grant effectiveness is to figure out what costs are involved and how best to use precious time to meet deadlines. Jane lists different types of grants: State Trails grant, State Parks grant, Federal Land and Water Conservation grants, and the N.C. Clean Water Management Trust Fund (CWMTF) grant; this last, the one she wrote for this portion of the New

Hope Creek Corridor. She can only write but so many grants, so it is imperative that she not squander time and efforts. Jane pre-scores the endangered species involved, the waterway that, damaged, can't be repaired, the educational assets, the amount of linear stream, the esthetic value. With all the different kinds of grants, she needs to assess exactly which is the most appropriate for the relevant circumstances.

Since the CWMTF grant program was instituted by Governor Jim Hunt in 1997, Durham County has applied for four grants and now has received four! Jane Korest has had many amazing successes, not the least of them the New Hope Creek Corridor. As she has explained, it was a textbook example of a project that could easily have failed, but also a textbook example of one that could win. This would be the highest price for open space that Durham has ever paid, with a developer already invested and the development process well along; but the people instrumental in our struggle made smart move after smart move. "No" was never taken as a final answer, although it was often stated. It all happened because of determination. Ideally a plan and vision should be in place, but in this case both formed and grew, with an ever-increasing momentum of support.

Wendy once asked Jane, "What could really make this work?" The answer was simple; namely, if the Board of Commissioners decides the project is a priority. But then, how, indeed, do you make it a manageable priority? Here the answers are many:

- ☼ Getting the other neighborhoods and towns involved removed a possible NIMBY concern because one of the region's backyards could gain in greenway and natural beauty.

- ☼ Partnerships are exciting to grantors; having a non-profit backing the effort helped legitimize and give our efforts credibility from the start.

- ☼ The internet e-mailing made the elected officials know how important it was to the citizens, who could not be ignored.

- ☼ Connecting it to children and their education introduced another whole aspect and great photo ops! (At this writing the new park is already being used as an outdoor classroom by Forest View Elementary.)

- The legislative tour created good will. Folks recognized they were backing a winner.

- Including four jurisdictions made it more affordable to each constituency.

And when it was really important to do so, Wendy shifted the focus to elected officials, those that could vote on our behalf. The support of the people was already in place. Democracy in action!

The Pennys's donating easements on their upper land was nice, but this was not the tract integral to the plan. Rather it was the flood plain of the Penny land. Wade was very savvy in stating that he would not budge without the Duke tract being included; this was the bargaining chip that turned the tide. This deal, along with EANG and TLC being the greatest contributors, gave more weight to the County's grant request, which was successfully awarded.

Jane's last piece of advice is to always take the high road and always give others the benefit of the doubt. She realizes this is hard for citizen activists to do, but acting otherwise can undercut what they wish to achieve. When she started out with Durham Planning Department in 1985, there were no provisions even for wildlife corridors. We have come a long way since then, but there is still a distance to go; for example, 250 more acres along the New Hope Creek corridor remain unprotected. As their availability becomes known, TLC will be contacting Jane. I suspect they have her number on their speed dial.

March 15, 2004 – Liz Carter and Ron Noel get an eviction notice. Carillon Developers have bought the Few families 102 acres and plan to develop it into 163 houses.

March 16, 2004 – Vickie West, neighbor to Liz and Ron secures plat map of proposed development from Planning Department.

March 25, 2004 – Representing the sub-division of Stonegate, Marty Galliano makes a strong articulate speech at the City Council work session, requesting one item; that the entrance of Carillon Forest avoid their neighborhood entirely.

March 25, 2004 – Lisa Cavanaugh - Duke graduate student, Alice Griffin - artist, Emily Weinstein (Em), Vickie, Ron - rock landscaper, Jessie Eustace, attend the same meeting as Ms. Galliano to request lower density, tree protection and to preserve the Pickett graveyard and farmhouse built in 1864.

March, 2004 – Em hiking on the Hollow Rock Trail meets Jeff Fisher, Executive Director of the Tar River Land Conservancy – she tells him of impending development. Em around this time tells Wade and Carolyn Penny of the Few Land sale and Liz and Ron's need to move.

April, 2004 – Next public hearing at City Hall Jeff, Lisa and Wendy make strong pitches for land protection. Alice presents a large portrait of the great Sycamore tree. Britt Spivey, the developer's rep asks to buy it to hang in show house.

April, 2004 – First meeting with Becky Heron, County Commissioner, with Jeff, Alice, Lisa, Wendy, Em and Chuck Eilber, neighbor. Erwin Association Neighborhood Group (EANG) is formed.

April, 2004 – At City Council public hearing, well attended by 3 neighborhoods. Mr. Spivey agrees with no entrance into Stonegate, some tree protection, will attempt to give away old house and protection for graveyard. Lower density he does not address. Soon after this meeting he moves to Texas.

May 1, 2004 – Liz and Ron move to Penny's old farmhouse transplanting 1000's of plants. Other tenant on the same land, David Southern, historian and Duke Press editor moves to Hildegard Ryals's large house.

May 2004 –Em sees surveyors chopping through Duke Forest. Forty-four acres are in negotiation with Crosland Developers. She alerts all.

May 2004 – Kim Forehand secures plat map from Planning Dept. EANG calls a meeting that is poorly attended.

May 2004 – Next EANG meeting the group quadruples in size. Em designs logo. Lisa insists on bumperstickers and road signs. Wendy picks a date to reserve the elementary school and strategies are in motion.

June 2004 – Maggie Peltier – creates an EANG website.

June 17, 2004 – Herald Sun "Road to Ruin? Erwin Rd Home Owners Wary of Plans to Build 425 Houses in a LIttle More Than a Mile"

June 18, 2004 – Lisa sends out an email with a strong message.

June 21, 2004 – Neighboring lands committee meeting at Solterra Common House with Becky Heron.

June 29, 2004 – Meeting neighboring lands committee, Solterra Common House.

July 22, 2004 – City Council Work Session meeting; plat approval "Carillon Subdivision" preliminary.

July 28, 2004 – EANG meeting with Carillon developer at Forest View Elementary School.

August 1, 2004 – Meeting EANG.

August 2, 2004 – Meeting City Council. Herald Sun "Growthzilla" editorial cartoon.

August 5, 2004 – Meeting Solterra homeowners with Jim Anderson of Crosland Developers.

September 15 & 20, 2004 – Meeting EANG.

September 26, 2004 – Solterra fall community meeting; Jeff Fisher. Presentation for EANG.

September 29, 2004 - EANG community meeting re Duke Tract and Carillon Development, held at Solterra Common House.

October 21 & 25, 2004 – Meeting EANG. Re: Crosland.

October 27, 2004 – Meeting EANG with Crosland's Jim Anderson, 14 present.

November 4, 2004 - EANG presents "Better Alternative" Plan to City Council Work Session.

November 5, 2004 – Herald Sun "City Asked to Prevent

Annexation of Tract."

November 5, 2004 – EANG attends DRB (Development Review Board) re: Crosland Developers.

Nov. 6, 2004 - Herald Sun "County Gets Shot at Duke Tract."

November 8, 2004 – EANG attends Durham County Community meeting to ask them to invoke 120 day reservation on Duke Tract.

November 9, 2004 – Herald Sun "County Votes to Reserve Duke Tract."

November 9, 2004 – EANG asks Joint City County Planning Commission to delay vote on extension of water & sewer.

November 12, 2004 – Herald Sun "Counties May be Partners on Park."

November 16, 2004 – EANG presents "Better Alternative" Plan to Orange County Commission.

November 17, 2004 – Chronical newspaper article "Don't Sell the Land" written by Wendy Jacobs and Lisa Cavanaugh.

November 24, 2004 – Herald Sun "Duke Wants $1.5 Million for Urban Road Tract."

November 28, 2004 – Herald Sun Editorial "Buy the land or Regret it!"

December 6, 2004 – Public annexation decision removed from city council agenda.

December 8, 2004 – Four months reservation date set.

January 25, 2005 – EANG kickoff at Forest View School: first public organizational meeting, videos of creek 7:00pm.

January 25, 2005 – 103 pledges of $35,704 raised.

February 1, 2005 – EANG meeting 7:30pm.

February 7, 2005 – Herald Sun "Locals: Which Way do We Grow?" about Arrowhead.

February 8, 2005 – Letter from the Pennys to 4 jurisdictions. $46,587 in pledges raised to date.

February 9, 2005 – Herald Sun "Park Splits Officials Managers." Carolyn and Wade Penny announce 60 acre free conservation easement contingent on the land being funded.

February 9, 2005 – EANG presents plan to Durham - Chapel Hill - Orange County work group. Penny's announce intention to protect their land if Duke land is protected.

February 17, 2005 – Herald Sun "Duke has dual responsibility with forest."

March 1, 2005 – $56,000 raised

March 5, 2005 – Walk/Talk starting at Solterra Club House.

March 9, 2005 – Herald Sun "Three-tiered Plan Proposed for Duke Land."

March 9, 2005 – EANG attends Durham-Chapel Hill-Orange County work group and asks for support for a regional park.

March 12, 2005 – Penny's announce sale of 25 acres at $5,000 an acre, about $30,000 each under market value.

March 24, 2005 – At the City Council Work Session TLC announces their offer to Durham of $25,000 towards the Park. TLC challenges EANG to raise $150,000 by April 1st.

April 4, 2005 – Durham County votes 3-2 for $900,000 contingent Orange County coming through with $200,000. Durham City Council votes Yes, 4-3 on $75,000 for Park.

April 5, 2005 – Herald Sun "Durham County Okays Erwin Trace Money If…"

April 6, 2005 – Chapel Hill votes 8-1 to contribute an additional $25,000 towards the Park.

April 7, 2005 – Herald Sun "Orange Secures Erwin Preserve." Orange County Commissioners vote Yes 4 to 1.

April 8, 2005 - Deadline! Last day of County reservation. Durham County signs contract with Duke.

April 19, 2005 – EANG 7:30pm meeting.

April 20, 2005 – Herald Sun letter from Mary Semans "Erwin Road Land Buy Shows Love of Nature."

April 22, 2005 – EANG still needs to raise $56,000.

April 26, 2005 – Herald Sun editorial and letter "More Fundraising Needed to Buy Erwin Road Land."

May 2, 2005 – Herald Sun Editorial "Better Planning Leads to Clean Air."

May 22, 2005 – Art for the Park benefit at Em's 2:00-6:00pm.

June 1, 2005 – CWMTF grant submitted by Jane Korest.

July 8, 2005 – Herald Sun "Group Closes in on Funds for Ex-Duke Forest Land," Great photo of Wendy.

July 15, 2005 – Herald Sun "Group Exceeds Goal to Save 42 Acre Tract." "Neighbors Raise $207,000 and County Will Kick in the Rest."

July 25, 2005 – 9:30-10:30 "Legislative Tour " by State and local officials of New Hope Creek Preserve - featured on NBC17-TV that night, with interviews with Wendy Jacobs, Wade Penny and Becky Heron

July 26, 2005 – Herald Sun "Preserving the Creek" 3 color photos - Bill Holman, Director of the CWMTF, standing on the Hollow Rock of the New Hope Creek Preserve, as well as picture of children holding "Thank you" signs to TLC, Duke Univ., Durham Co., Orange Co., Chapel Hill and City of Durham.

July 29, 2005 – Herald Sun "Erwin Trace Park Planning Begins."

July 2005 – TLC News "Opportunity Knocks in New Hope Corridor – Local Communities EANG and TLC Answer."

October 14, 2005 – Herald Sun "State Wants More Information on Land Deal at Erwin, Pickett Roads."

November 15, 2005 – $1.2 million CWMTF grant approved by the board. Jane Korest attends 2 days of meetings in Wilmington, NC.

Flyer for first public EANG event
Designed & written by Mary Peterson

COMPLETE THE PUZZLE!

Help Create New Hope Creek Park in West Durham

Join the Erwin Area Neighborhood Group's (EANG) grass roots campaign to help purchase the Duke tract at the corner of Erwin and Pickett roads for public open space and recreational use for the citizens of Durham and Orange counties. Durham County is currently looking into acquiring this property for the community and they need our support. Orange County, Durham City and Chapel Hill have also expressed interest in a regional park.

WHAT: New Hope Creek Park - Campaign Kickoff Event
WHEN: Tuesday, January 25, 2005
TIME: 7:00pm - 8:30pm
WHERE: Forest View Elementary School
(corner of Mt. Sinai and Erwin Road, Durham)

What you can expect:

✳Meet your elected officials and find out about Durham County's 120 day reservation on the property;

✳Learn how this property will add to the New Hope Creek Corridor Master Plan...a walking trail that will stretch from the Hollow Rock area down to Jordan Lake and benefit all;

✳Find out how you can help make New Hope Creek Park become a reality;

✳Participate in The Yard Sale...the yard here being the Duke tract...your pledge will help the community purchase this forest land for public use.

For more information contact the EANG at geewen@nc.rr.com
website: www.erwinneighbor.org

PLEASE FORWARD THIS INVITATION TO YOUR FRIENDS AND NEIGHBORS. CHILDREN ARE WELCOME!

❖ Key Players ❖

Marc Alperin – Author's supportive boyfriend.

Bill Bell – Mayor of Durham.

Sandy Bisdee – EANG member, arranged concert fundraiser.

Kevin Brice – Director of Triangle Land Conservancy.

Eugene Brown – Durham City Council member.

CWMTF – Clear Water Management Trust Fund

Diane Catotti – Durham City Council member.

Lisa Cavanaugh – PhD student, EANG spokesperson

Deb Christie – Organizer of EANG events & database.

Cora Cole-McFadden – Durham City Council, cast deciding vote.

Ken Coulter - New Hope Creek Corridor Advisory

Reverend Phil Cousin – Durham County commissioner.

Taymon Domzalski – M.D. student, Lisa's partner, EANG

Frank Duke – Durham Planning Director.

Judson Edeburn – Duke Forest Resource Manager

Chuck Eilber – educator, original EANG member.

Jessie Johnson Eustice – Tommy Thompson's daughter, lived on Few property 1965-1976.

Jeff Fisher – Originator of Tar River Conservancy, EANG leader.

Kim Forehand – Naturalist, tour guide, EANG member.

Walter Fowler – Longtime supporter of New Hope Creek, original NHCCAC member.

Kevin Foy – Mayor of Chapel Hill.

Mike Giles – Dur. Co. Open Space, works with Jane Korest.

Alice Gordon - Orange county commissioner

Layne Gothard – EANG member, designed petition.

Steve Halkiotis – Orange county commissioner

Ed Harrison – Chapel Hill town council member, helped write 1991 New Hope Creek Master Plan.

Becky Heron – Durham county commissioner.

Bill Holman – Exec. Dir. Clear Water Management trust fund.

Buck Horton – EANG member, wrote long comprehensive column for the Independent Weekly.

Barry Jacobs – Orange County Commissioner

Wendy Jacobs – spokesperson and strategist for EANG.

Eliza, Caleb, Zachery J. Meredith – EANG event & art dept. volunteers (Wendy's progeny).

John Kent – New Hope Creek stream watch, Sierra Club.

Jane Korest – Durham Open Space and Real Estate Manager. Author of major land grants.

Phil & Nancy Leinbach – Brochure/refreshment crew for EANG events

Joe Liles – artist/teacher – Donated large silk screened prints of the New Hope Creek to raise funds.

Doug & Susan MacKinnon – EANG brochure and attended all meetings.

Tom Magnuson – Dir. of Trading Path Assoc., historian.

Jeff Masten – Works with Kevin Brice of TLC

Jon and Beatrice Miller – EANG members that held plant sale fundraiser.

Kevin McPeak – Designed EANG on-line pledge system.

Alice Griffin Myers – EANG art dept., support A to Z

Ron Noel & Liz Carter – Lived in antebellum farm house on Few land, moved to Rose-Penny homestead.

Bill Olive – Longtime supporter of New Hope Creek, original NHCCAC member.

Maggie Peltier – originator of EANG website.

Carolyn Penny – bought Rose property with husband Wade in 1986, donated it into trust 2005.

Wade Penny – lawyer, activist – former Durham City Council member and former State Legislator member.

Mary Peterson – EANG, designed flyer and wrote key letters.

Randy Pickle – managed EANG website.

Ellen Reckhow – chair Durham County Commission, developed agreement for 4 jurisdictions.

Bernice & Gertrude Rose – Bought the land in 1965, that in 2005 more than doubled the New Hope greenway.

Lu Rose – EANG member

Hildegard Ryals – chair New Hope Creek Corridor Advisory Committee (NHCCAC), EANG member.

Rich Shaw – manager of the Orange Co. Lands Legacy Prog.

David Southern – lived in Pickett house on Few land after T. Thompson and family moved out, local historian.

Bill Strom – Chapel Hill town Council member.

Tommy Thompson – original Red Clay Rambler, lived in Pickett house on Few property.

Tallman Trask III – Executive Vice President, Duke Univ.

Mary Margaret Wade - Designer of our Burma-shave type signs

Don Weil – manager EANG listserv for massive e-mail alerts.

Sally Weil – macrobiotic EANG baker.

Emily Weinstein – Whistle blower, EANG art dept.

Vickie West – Lives across from Few land, helped with art fundraiser

Local

Ellerbe Creek

www.ellerbecreek.org

Dedicated to restoring Ellerbe Creek, Durham, NC by restoring native plant and wildlife habitat, open space and water quality. Our long term goal is a series of preserves connected by trails along the length of the creek that allow people to connect with nature by simply walking or biking from their homes and work places. We do stormwater management, installation and maintenance of wetland gardens, trail building, stream and native plant restoration, public education and working with landowners and government agencies to preserve and protect land and water.

Eno River Association

www.enoriver.org

Dedicated to conserving and protecting the nature, culture, and history of the Eno River Basin since 1966. The Eno River Festival helps in funding the acquisition of land surrounding the Eno River. The festival takes place during the 4th of July weekend and showcases music of every kind, dancing, crafts and non-profits. A not-to-be-missed event!

Friends of Bolin Creek

www.bolincreek.org

The Friends of Bolin Creek is a non-profit organization dedicated to preserving the Bolin Creek corridor by working with the University of North Carolina, the towns of Chapel Hill and Carrboro, and with Orange County. We would like to establish a perpetual nature park, and preserve the Bolin Creek Watershed. We envision multiple uses compatible with our preservation goals, including hiking, biking, birding and nature study.

New Hope Creek Corridor Advisory Committee

www.newhopecreek.org

New Hope Creek is a narrow waterway that snakes its way from western Orange County, North Carolina, passing north of Chapel Hill and through parts of Durham, finally emptying into the upper reaches of Jordan Lake. In 1989, four local jurisdictions passed a resolution recognizing the importance of preserving the creek, its tributaries and a corridor along their banks. The New Hope Corridor Open Space Master Plan was developed and the New Hope Creek Corridor Advisory Committee was established to advise the local governments on implementing the plan.

The Committee maintains this website to report on its progress and to invite the public to explore and help preserve the beautiful New Hope Creek corridor.

Triangle Land Conservancy

www.tlc-nc.org

TLC is the land trust for a six-county region including Chatham, Durham, Johnston, Lee, Orange and Wake Counties (NC). TLC protects important open space—stream corridors, forests, wildlife habitat, farmland and natural areas—to help keep our region a healthy and vibrant place to live and work.

In-State

Clean Water for North Carolina

www.cwfnc.org

We help communities get organized, develop strategies and take action against pollution. We research to strengthen enforcement for community protection, and enhancing citizen control of local and state environment. We can work with you to review permits, document violations, or even to get commitments from a polluter in your community.

Clean Water Management Trust Fund

www.cwmtf.net

Created in 1996, the Clean Water Management Trust Fund makes grants to local governments, state agencies and conservation non-profits to help finance projects that specifically address water-pollution problems.

Conservation Trust for North Carolina

www.ctnc.org

CTNC is the umbrella organization for the state's network of 23 local land trusts. The Conservation Trust works in partnership with local land trusts, private landowners, public agencies and concerned citizens to ensure that critical lands are voluntarily protected for clean drinking water, recreation, tourism, and working forests and farms. CTNC also works directly with landowners, local land trusts and government agencies to protect land along the Blue Ridge Parkway's natural and scenic corridor.

Environmental Enhancement Program

www.nceep.net

The N.C. Ecosystem Enhancement Program combines an existing wetlands-restoration initiative by the N.C. Department of Environment and Natural Resources with ongoing environmental efforts by the N.C. Department of Transportation. The U.S. Army Corps of Engineers joined as a sponsor in the historic agreement.

Environment North Carolina

www.environmentnorthcarolina.org

Environment North Carolina is a statewide, citizen-based environmental advocacy organization. The staff combines independent research, practical ideas and tough-minded advocacy to overcome the opposition of powerful special interests and win real results for North Carolina's environment.

Land for Tomorrow

www.landfortomorrow.org

Land for Tomorrow is a statewide partnership of conservationists, farmers, business leaders, local governments, health professionals and community groups urging the General Assembly to provide $1 billion over five years to protect the state's land, water and special places before they are irreversibly lost.

Million Acre Initiative

www.onencnaturally.org

With an end goal of preserving one million additional acres of open space in North Carolina this decade, the Million Acre Initiative coordinates preservation efforts between a number of organizations — federal, state and local governments, conservation groups and citizens. While supporting existing programs, the initiative also encourages cooperation by providing technical assistance and information to people interested in helping our state meet its goal.

Mountain Voices Alliance

www.mvalliance.net

The majestic mountains of western North Carolina are at risk. Mountain Voices works to preserve and protect the environment, including the natural beauty, abundant resources, quality of life and cultural heritage of our communities. We achieve our goals by working with local governments, developers, organizations and individuals to encourage responsible and sustainable development that is in the best interest of citizens, visitors and future generations.

Natural Heritage Trust Fund

www.ncnhtf.org

The Natural Heritage Trust Fund is a funding source for state agencies to acquire and protect land with outstanding natural or cultural heritage value. These land acquisitions become additions to state parks, state trails, aesthetic forests, game lands, historical sites, etc., and are then used for recreational, scientific, educational, cultural and aesthetic purposes. Grants are also made for natural area inventories and conservation planning.

NC Agricultural Development and Farmland Preservation Trust Fund

www.ncadfp.org

North Carolina lost 1 million acres of forestland between 1990 and 2002, three quarters of this loss to urban development. Since 2002, North Carolina has lost more than 6,000 farms and 300,000 acres of farmland. This puts us in the unenviable position of leading the nation in farm loss. NCADFP is working to slow, if not stop, that statistic.

The N.C. Division of Parks and Recreation

www.ncsparks.gov

We have a beautiful park system which residents can help support by getting a NC state parks license plate. In addition to supporting our Naturally Wonderful state parks system by displaying this very attractive license plate, a portion of the sale will benefit the parks and recreation and the natural heritage trust funds.

NC Green Power

www.ncgreenpower.com

NCGP was established to improve North Carolina's environment through voluntary contributions toward renewable energy. The goal is to supplement the state's existing power supply with more green energy – electricity generated from renewable resources like the sun, wind and organic matter. Citizens agreeing to pay as little as $4.00 a month fund this program…. The author does.

North Carolina Rail-Trails

www.ncrail-trails.org

Our abandoned railroad tracks are being transformed into a linear park system throughout the United States. They are the most cost-effective way to provide safe, off-road hiking, bicycling, skating and saddle riding facilities for a community or region.

The North Carolina Sustainable Energy Association

www.ncsustainableenergy.org

Through multiple exciting programs NCSEA works with their members, government, business and partner organizations to provide communication outlets, information and opportunities for North Carolinians to learn about and use sustainable energy solutions.

NC WARN – Waste Awareness and Reduction Network
www.ncwarn.org
A grassroots non-profit watchdog group using science and activism to tackle climate change and reduce hazards to public health and the environment from nuclear power and other polluting electricity production, and working for a transition to safe, economical energy in North Carolina.

Parks and Recreation Trust Fund
www.partf.net
PARTF is the primary source of funding to build and renovate facilities in the state parks as well as to buy land for new and existing parks. The PARTF program also provides dollar-for-dollar grants to local governments. Recipients use the grants to acquire land and/or to develop parks and recreational projects that serve the general public.

Southern Energy and Environment Expo
www.seeexpo.com
This annual event held at the Western N.C. Agricultural Center in Fletcher, NC, is designed to showcase renewable energy and sustainable economics in a context of responsible environmental stewardship.

National

Audubon
www.audubon.org
Audubon has been a leader in the conservation of the birds of the United States. The threats today are far different from those of a century ago, but Audubon's commitment is as strong as ever. The mission of the National Audubon Society is to conserve and restore natural ecosystems, focusing on birds, other wildlife and their habitats for the benefit of humanity and to preserve biological diversity.

Big Box Tool Kit, *Countering Mega-Retailers – Rebuilding Local Business*
www.bigboxtoolkit.com
They can assist you in working to prevent sprawl caused by big box stores. This is a project of the Institute for Local Self-Reliance, a national nonprofit organization to advance sustainable, equitable and community-centered economic development through research, educational activities and technical assistance.

Community & Environmental Defense Services
www.ceds.org
CEDS exists solely to help people defend their community and environment from the impact of sprawl, bad zoning decisions and other flawed development projects. If you are seeking advice on how to protect your home or neighborhood from poorly planned growth, then contact us at 1-800-773-4571 or Help@ceds.org. Our advice is available free to citizens advocating a responsible development plan.

The Conservation Fund
www.conservationfund.org
They are a nonprofit dedicated to protecting America's landscapes and waterways. Through its partnership-driven approach, the Fund works across all 50 states to preserve each region's unique natural resources, cultural heritage and historic places. Committed to effectiveness, efficiency and environmental and economic balance, the Fund is pioneering a new environmentalism that is results-oriented and sustainable, agile and inclusive.

End Mountaintop Removal
www.ilovemountains.org
Visit this site to learn what action is being taken to save our mountains from coal mining and how you can help.

Green Power Partnership
www.epa.gov/greenpower/
Across America consumers increasingly have a choice when they buy electricity. With that choice comes the ability to buy green power. Green power is an environmentally friendly electricity product that is generated from renewable energy sources. Buying green power is easy, and it offers benefits over conventional electricity. EPA's Green Power Partnership provides assistance and recognition to organizations that demonstrate environmental leadership by choosing green power.

Land Trust Alliance
www.ltanet.org/findlandtrust
This comprehensive list of land trusts in the United States is helpful in locating a non-profit to possibly underwrite your conservation projects.

National Arbor Day Foundation

www..arborday.org

This group inspires people to plant, nurture, and celebrate trees. They envision a world where trees and forests are abundant, healthy, and sustainable, and highly valued by all people.

The Nature Conservancy

www.nature.org

The mission of The Nature Conservancy is to preserve the plants, animals and natural communities that represent the diversity of life on Earth by protecting the lands and waters they need in order to survive.

Scenic America – Change is inevitable. Ugliness is not.

www.scenic.org

SA works to reduce billboard blight in America, keep highways and byways scenic, promote scenic easements for open space and scenic resource conservation, promote tree conservation and undergrounding of overhead utility wires.

Sierra Club

www.sierraclub.org

The Sierra Club's members are more than 750,000 of your friends and neighbors. Inspired by nature, we work together to protect our communities and the planet. The Club is America's oldest, largest and most influential grassroots environmental organization.

Southern Environmental Law Center

www.southernenvironment.org

For the past 20 years, the Southern Environmental Law Center has used the full power of the law to conserve clean water, healthy air, wild lands and livable communities throughout the Southeast. As the biggest, most powerful environmental organization headquartered in the South, SELC is able to work simultaneously in all three branches of government, and in all of our six focus states, to comprehensively address the most urgent problems facing our region.

Trading Path Association

www.tradingpath.org

In order to conserve the archeology of England's first frontier, the Trading Path Association finds and protects Indian trails and colonial roads. It encourages local governments to make early colonial landscapes into heritage tourism assets, thus making them more valuable undeveloped than developed. The goal is to preserve our common past from the onslaught of sprawl.

Trees Are Good

www.treesaregood.org

This web site provides excellent tree care information. If you have a question, they can answer it with expert and respectful advice. They can also help you find a local ISA Certified Arborist.

Publications

Back Home Magazine

www.backhomemagazine.com

A magazine that delivers useful do-it-yourself information on sustainable, self-reliant living. Since 1990, *Back Home* has been the authority for those interested in taking control of their own lives. The bimonthly issues are packed with proven information and resources on rural land, mortgage-free building, solar and renewable energy, chemical free gardening, wholesome cooking, home business, home-schooling, small livestock, vehicle and workshop projects, and family activities.

The Duke Forest at 75: *A Resource for All Seasons* by Ida Phillips Lynch.... The Office of the Duke Forest's comprehensive history involving the Forest. From origins, research projects, the characters involved and more are captured with interesting text and many photos.

The Earth Remains Forever: *Generations at a Crossroads* by Rob Jackson.... Lays out the scientific facts in plain language and with flashes of humor. Jackson shows how the escalation of population growth and resource consumption in the twentieth century caused problems from ozone depletion to global warming, habitat destruction and biodiversity loss. He highlights ongoing solutions to these problems and ways in which we can create a sustainable future for subsequent generations and all life on earth. His urgent message is not that we've already failed, but that we can succeed.

Last Child in the Woods: *Saving Our Children from Nature-Deficit Disorder* by Richard Louv.... The author talks with parents, children, teachers, scientists, religious leaders, child-development researchers, and environmentalists who recognize the threat and offer solutions. Louv shows us an alternative future, one in which parents help their kids experience the natural world more deeply — and find the joy of family connectedness in the process.

The Last Landscape by William H. Whyte.... Called "the best study available on the problems of open space" by the New York Times when it first appeared in 1968, *The Last Landscape* introduced many cornerstone ideas for land conservation, urging all of us to make better use of the land that has survived amid suburban sprawl. Whyte's pioneering work on easements led to the passage of major open- space statutes in many states, and his argument for using and linking green spaces, however small the areas may be, is a recommendation that has more currency today than ever before.

Mother Earth News
www.motherearthnews.com
Each issue of *Mother Earth News* is packed with organic-gardening advice, do-it-yourself projects, renewable energy options and hands-on ways you can enjoy and protect natural resources. The magazine and its websites offer practical ideas for saving energy, eating real food, and pursuing natural health, self-sufficiency and much more.

Orion Magazine
www.orionmagazine.org
The Orion Society currently furthers its mission through three fundamental programs: the ideas and inspiration of *Orion Magazine*, community activism through the Orion Grassroots Network, and environmental teaching through Orion Education.

A Sand County Almanac by Aldo Leopold.... Admired by an ever-growing number of readers and imitated by hundreds of writers, this classic continues to inspire thought and action as more citizens grapple with matters of conservation and sustainability more than ever before. Melding science and philosophy in his beautiful prose, Leopold calls on each of us to develop an ecological conscience and contribute to weaving a land ethic into our culture.

Silent Spring by Rachel Carson.... First published in 1962, *Silent Spring* alerted a large audience to the environmental and human dangers of indiscriminate use of pesticides, spurring revolutionary changes in the laws affecting our air, land, and water. The book is widely credited with launching the environmentalism movement in the West and facilitated the ban of the pesticide DDT in 1972 in the United States.

Photo by Alice Griffin

❖ About the Author ❖

EMILY EVE WEINSTEIN moved to North Carolina in 1982, and has become known for her murals, portraits of people and pets and exhibiting fine art. Her other books to date are *Moon Book*, published by Discovery Press, and *Cat Book* and *Dog Book*, both released by Beau Soleil Publishing.

❖ Em's Readymade Studio ❖

The Ready-Made Studio consists of a five-gallon bucket with an indented lid used as a pallet. A flat piece of plexiglass has been cut to fit as a cover for the paints. Duct tape holds the lid in place when the artist slogs through one kind of terrain or another.

The bucket carries the brushes (protected by a paper towel roll), rags, non-toxic painting medium in artichoke jar stabilized in small-truck hubcap, tube of white oil paint, and some pieces of primed reclaimed wood surfaces to paint on.

www.WeinsteinArt.com